CAL ALLEY

CAL ALLEY

edited by Charles W. Crawford

foreword by Jack Knox

afterword by Frank R. Ahlgren

MEMPHIS State University Press

Library of Congress Catalog number: 72–82797
International Standard Book Number: 0–87870–013–7
Cartoons reprinted by permission of *The Commercial Appeal*.

Manufactured by Memphis State University Printing Services.

To My Parents

ACKNOWLEDGEMENTS

In preparing a book an author usually incurs obligations. I am no exception. Many people have provided invaluable aid and encouragement in the preparation of this book and I wish to take this opportunity to express my gratitude to them. The person whose early vision of a book on this subject inspired me with the same conviction was Mr. James Simmons, the editor of the Memphis State University Press. Without his foresight this work probably would not have developed. A special note of thanks is due to Ms. Rosie Eberle, who as associate editor of the university press, aided in the early planning of the book. Her judicious counsel has been given also in the latter stages of preparation even though she was not then associated with the press.

A number of friends and professional associates have given advice and encouragement in this work and although I do not attempt to list them here I hope they will understand my appreciation. The patient indulgence of my family in accepting an author's eccentricities has contributed to the completion of this task, and I owe a special debt to my son, Larry, who served as proofreader for the manuscript. His newspaper editorial experience and his own writing ability, which certainly surpasses that of his university professor father, has received my absolute trust. Dr. Johnye E. Mathews, editor, author, and chairman of the Department of English of the University of Arkansas at Little Rock, has read all of the manuscript and made invaluable suggestions for its improvement.

There are several sources of whatever understanding the author may have of the region for which *The Commercial Appeal* is a spokesman. It has been my good fortune to be allowed to share the ideas of several historians whose fascination with the South has equalled mine. I owe much to William Doherty, now at West Virginia University, James Silver, presently at the University of South Florida, and the late Enoch L. Mitchell. The John Willard Brister Library of Memphis State University has generously supplied from their microfilm collection copies of Cal Alley cartoons which were not included in the family files. Dewey Pruett, Curator of the Mississippi Valley Collection of this library, has supplied much information from his excellent archive. I also am indebted to the Oral History Research Office of Memphis State University for information from its regional collection, and to Dr. Cecil C. Humphreys, under whose leadership this office was established. Furthermore, my many students of Tennessee history have taught me much (probably without knowing that they were teaching me) with their penetrating and persistent comments and questions. We have learned together and I appreciate the experience.

Last, though not so in importance, I wish to express my gratitude to Mrs. Calvin Alley and her children. Without interfering in any way with my freedom to reach my own conclusions and state them as I wished, they have supplied every aid and courtesy that any scholar could wish. The opportunity to know this close and loyal southern family has enhanced my understanding of Cal Alley's world. Any errors of fact or interpretation in the text of this book are my own.

FOREWORD

When a cartoonist lays out his work he should have something to say, to say forcefully. Perhaps his cartoon should clarify a complicated issue. Or at times, when a situation calls, it should touch the heart. But most effectively, perhaps, a cartoon is able to carry a political message, the kind of message that can stick in the craws of politicians and stick in the minds of newspaper readers.

These aims are accomplished, sometimes, by the use of comparisons—simplified pictorial parables. Or by pathos that depends almost entirely on the character and ability of the draftsman. Too, there is the pointing up of the irony in given situations and issues.

But in the field of politics the editorial cartoonist is at his best. Such cartoons are the true test of his sense of humor, both in thought and drawing. In this field the cartoonist's best work has been described as "graphic satire."

A former President of the United States, speaking of the Society of American Editorial Cartoonists (150 qualified members, maybe) said that no other body so small, excepting the Senate of the United States, has carried as much influence in the thinking and workings of this nation at the grassroots. And he is right, most probably, and is backed up by the accomplishments of the profession set down in the chronicles of time and the world.

Cal Alley was a good, sound thinker, mentally sharp and alert, possessing, in a sense, the mind of an editor, able to pick the proper subject for the day, go to the heart of it, and give it the right treatment, the right slant, the proper timing. He had mastered an excellent drawing technique, but his character, his heart, his sense of humor always "showed through." An extremely fast worker, Cal Alley could produce in minutes a cartoon that would require most cartoonists hours to produce. And with his quickness, perhaps because of it, his drawings conveyed a freshness, a pen and ink and brush boldness, a distinctive character and personality that any practicing member of the profession could envy.

He was once asked, "How long does it take to produce a cartoon?"

His truthful answer: "Ten hours and twenty minutes!"

"Huh?"

"Ten hours to work up the idea, twenty minutes to draw it."

The late, great J. P. Alley once told me; "Anyone who pays a nickel for *The Commercial Appeal* should understand your cartoon, should get the point of it . . . even if he hasn't seen a newspaper in twenty years. Remember, you're drawing for those fellows down on the levee, for the groceryman, the banker, the barber, the machinist, the farmer. You're not drawing to please some New York or London editor who'll reprint your stuff."

Cal Alley "grew up" in the editorial cartooning profession, aiming and developing his mind toward it from early childhood. He heeded to the letter the sound advice, the helpful suggestions, the wise criticisms of his illustrious father, who was a masterful, internationally famous cartoonist. Cal Alley was a cartoonist who preferred drawing for his "own kind of folks" and had the courage to wave aside handsome offers by distant newspapers and famous editors.

In appreciating Cal Alley's "natural ability," knowing the strenuous effort and harsh self-discipline he gave unflaggingly to his work, it is difficult for an admirer to hold himself in check, to resist "Flingin' the language around," as J. P. might have put it. This collection of Cal Alley's work will stand solidly without props, as an accurate history of an era described quickly, though with the perception and skill of a great writer—for the pen is quicker than the type!

According to various researchers if a cartoonist's work doesn't catch the eye of a reader in three seconds, the cartoonist has lost him. If his work does catch the eye, the reader may glance at the cartoon eight or ten seconds, or he may study it with appreciation and amusement for ten minutes, or maybe cut it out for his scrap book.

The work of Cal Alley has caught the eye of more readers, informed more of them, swayed more of them, than any cartoonist I have known. And as a member of the profession for forty years, I have known them all—as personal friends or by their work. And although I had a few years start on Cal Alley (I always called him Calvin) I have always been proud to tip my hat and cheer this second illustrious Alley, an editorial cartoonist who, more frequently than not, beat me at my own game.

JACK KNOX
Nashville

Contents

INTRODUCTION

Calvin Lane Alley was born October 10, 1915, in Memphis, Tennessee. His parents, James Pinckney Alley and Nona Lane Alley, lived near the city where James Alley worked as an artist and as an editorial cartoonist for *The Commercial Appeal*. Calvin's childhood was spent in the Alley household with his parents, two sisters, and a brother, James Pinckney Alley, Jr. Calvin was the youngest of the children. Their home, a white board house near the intersection of Holmes and Summer, which was several miles outside of the city limits at that time, was destroyed by fire when Calvin was seven years old. As a result, the family moved to a new house on South Highland Street.

While the children were growing up, J. P. Alley became the first person to hold the position of daily cartoonist for *The Commercial Appeal*. Before Calvin was ten years old his father had received much of the honor for the Pulitzer prize awarded to the newspaper in 1923 for service displayed in its "courageous attitude in the publication of cartoons and the handling of news in reference to the operations of the Ku Klux Klan." Soon afterward one of his cartoons dealing with the Teapot Dome scandal and the presidential election of 1924 was given national distribution by the Democratic National Committee. J. P. Alley's cartoons were reprinted by many large newspapers, and his homespun Negro philosopher, "Hambone," created in 1915, was syndicated during the 1920's to a national audience of readers.

It is not surprising that under the influence of a successful and creative father both Calvin and his brother, Jim, became interested in cartooning. The time of Calvin's childhood included World War I, the twenties, and the beginning of the great depression. During all of this time he lived in Memphis, where his early education was acquired. He attended Treadwell and Messick Elementary Schools and Messick High School. When he graduated from Messick his father was seriously ill with Hodgkin's disease, and Calvin remained in Memphis, attending State

Teachers College (now Memphis State University) in that city in 1934. He was later called Cal by newer friends and professional acquaintances and his cartoons carried the signature "Cal Alley," although he remained Calvin to his family and early friends. After his father's death the following spring, he enrolled at Louisiana State University at Baton Rouge, but attended it only for a short time. He went next to Chicago where he studied at the American Academy of Arts in 1935–1936. Deciding to continue his study of art under different circumstances, he left the United States and spent the summer traveling and practicing his sketching in Mexico. His formal study of art resumed the following year when he enrolled in the Chicago Academy of Fine Arts.

Formal education, though, provided only part of Cal Alley's knowledge of and skill in cartooning. As a result of his father's illness he took up regular work in drawing at the age of eighteen, before he went away from home to study. Prior to his death J. P. Alley gave ownership of the syndicated cartoon feature "Hambone" to his wife, Nona, who continued to collect ideas and sayings for the cartoons and paid her artistically talented sons, Jim and Cal, to do the necessary drawing. Cal and his brother thus began a partnership that continued over two decades, each one of them drawing the daily panel cartoons every other week. Although there were individual characteristics of each brother's work, their depiction of Hambone was quite similar, and it is probable that many readers of the widely syndicated cartoon never realized that it was drawn by two different artists.

His share of the work involved in continuing the Alley family enterprise, "Hambone," provided Cal with regular, paid employment from the age of eighteen. The death of his father thus thrust adult responsibilities on him at an early age. It must have been a source of satisfaction to J. P. Alley during his final illness to realize that he had created a profitable cartoon character to be left to his family and that his sons had the talent and the interest to continue it. Wishing to get more varied cartooning experience than that involved in his share of the Hambone cartoons, Cal continued to study and to practice his drawing. In 1939, at the age of twenty-three, he secured his first regular work as a cartoonist for the Kansas City (Missouri) *Journal*. After working in this position for several months he returned to Memphis to marry Geraldine "Sissy" Jehl. The wedding took place November 28, 1939, and the couple moved to Kansas City where Cal continued to serve the *Journal* as cartoonist until the demise of that newspaper in 1942. During their residence in Kansas City two daughters were born, Jerrianne and Carol Lee. After the failure of the Kansas City newspaper he returned to Tennessee to become editorial cartoonist for the *Nashville Banner*. During these war-time years the Alleys' first son, Calvin Lane, Jr., was born. Although Cal Alley had found his life's work, he had not yet settled in the location he wished.

The management of *The Commercial Appeal* understandably had followed the career of the son of J. P. Alley, and was favorably impressed with his talent and professional development. Accordingly, in the Spring of 1945 he received a request to return to his home town to fill the position first held by his father—editorial cartoonist for the Memphis newspaper. Thomas H. Baker, the historian of *The Commercial Appeal*, gives the following statement about the decade following the death of J. P. Alley: "The *Commercial Appeal* hired other editorial cartoonists, but it would not have one to rival Alley's skill for more than ten years, when Calvin took his father's old job." The decision to accept the offer was not a difficult one for Cal to make. In April of that year he and his family moved back to Memphis, which was to be his home for the remainder of his life.

The return to Memphis was a homecoming to Cal and Sissy, as it had been their childhood home and both had relatives still living in the city. Their family continued to grow as two more children were born, Irene Jehl in 1948 and Richard Wesley in 1950. In 1949 the family moved to a comfortable home in a large, tree shaded lot at 3943 Poplar Avenue. Here all of the children grew to adulthood, and Cal himself spent many pleasant hours at the spacious, well lighted house, working at his drawings in several of the rooms.

Much of the warmth and hospitality of this home on Poplar Avenue found public expression in Alley drawings. Following a conversation with Sissy, in which they discussed the importance of a man's achieving success before his fortieth birthday, Cal Alley decided to begin a completely new artistic undertaking. In addition to his success in editorial cartooning for his newspaper and his continuing work on the syndicated "Hambone," he created a new family comic strip, "The Ryatts." The members of the Ryatt family closely resembled those of the Alley family and knowledgable acquaintances thought they had no difficulty in identifying the various Alleys in the drawings. Ideas and situations for "The Ryatts" were supplied regularly by members of the Alley family as well as by friends and by readers who contributed suggestions. The comic strip was syndicated by Post Hall (later, The Hall) Syndicate, starting in twenty-four newspapers in October, 1954—a year before Cal Alley's fortieth birthday. It is interesting to note that the contemporary comic strip "Pogo" started in four newspapers, and "Dennis the Menace" in six.

"The Ryatts" was quickly adopted by several hundred other papers, most of them in the United States. For thirteen years he continued to work on this new feature, but its extensive success created a problem. Producing the daily comic strip was a full time job requiring a great deal of work and involving a constant meeting of deadlines. In order to have time for this work he gave up his share of the work on "Hambone" soon after "The Ryatts" appeared, but by the time the first ten-year contract with the syndicate expired it was apparent that the work required in the editorial cartooning and drawing the comic strip was too great for one person to handle. Accordingly, Cal Alley ended his work on "The Ryatts" in 1967 to devote full time to *The Commercial Appeal*. The comic strip, however, was continued in syndication, and still recounts the experiences of a family which resembles the original Ryatt family.

Despite the great success of "The Ryatts," the decision to give it up was not a difficult one to make. Cal Alley had stated when he developed the comic strip that he would never give up editorial cartooning. It was always his first love professionally, and it rewarded him with numerous honors and widespread public acclaim. He received the awards modestly and appreciated critical as well as favorable comment. For instance, in 1949 an international controversy developed over one of his cartoons which was reprinted in the British *Sunday Pictorial*. In it John Bull appeared as a beggar holding a cup for a handout while standing in front of the Socialism Bar. The *London Daily Mail* referred to it as ". . . the now notorious cartoon," and Roy W. Howard, president of Scripps-Howard Newspaper Alliance, publicly apologized for the drawing which had come to the attention of the unhappy British public. Cal Alley, however, appreciated the controversy and had no apologies to make for the cartoon.

Other drawings won a different sort of recognition. The best known of these was one first published in the July 6, 1954, edition of *The Commercial Appeal*. It was the unanimous selection of fifty judges in 1955 for a Sigma Delta Chi award. Showing a ghostly American soldier wearing an arm band labeled "Korean Dead" and blocking the path of a bloody-handed figure of Red China as it advanced toward the United Nations, the cartoon was captioned "Over My Dead Body." This slogan undoubtedly expressed the feelings of many Americans, and Communist China did remain excluded from the U. N. through the remainder of Cal Alley's life.

Other honors were also received by the cartoons. Originals of some of them were requested by numerous well known Americans, including Franklin D. Roosevelt, Harry S. Truman, J. Edgar Hoover, Bernard Baruch, James F. Byrnes, Adlai Stevenson, and Dwight D. Eisenhower. Lyndon Johnson had a Cal Alley cartoon, the one showing the Democratic donkey grazing in Johnson grass while the Republican elephants fought one another, displayed at the opening of the Johnson Library at Austin, Texas. Several of the drawings from *The Commercial Appeal* were nominated for Pulitzer Prizes.

Considerable acclaim was also given to Cal Alley personally. Two chapters of "Quill and Scroll," a national journalism organization, at White Station High School and Immaculate Conception High School, were named for him. He was honored also by having one of his drawings of Uncle Sam selected for use in selling U. S. Savings Bonds after World War II. Another of his originals was displayed in a month-long exhibit of the work of contemporary cartoonists in

1952. Throughout the decade of the 1960's his work received approving attention from a private patriotic organization, Freedoms Foundation at Valley Forge, Pennsylvania. Seven medals and one certificate of merit were awarded to him by this foundation. Other awards were presented to him by the American Heart Association, the American Cancer Society, the Memphis and Shelby County Safety Council, the Memphis Urban League, and many other service and charitable organizations.

This extensive production of creative work was not accomplished without effort. It was fortunate that Cal Alley loved his work, for its demands were both exacting and unceasing. The 5:00 P.M. deadline when the daily editorial cartoon was due became a demanding taskmaster which regulated all his activity. And this deadline was almost always met. There were many times when he approached the time with steadily increasing pressure and no cartoon. There were some days when the deadline came and he had not been able to prepare a cartoon, thus finding it necessary to clip one from another newspaper. Occasionally also he submitted drawings that he considered to be inferior to his usual standards. Almost always, though, he met his deadlines successfully.

The most difficult challenge of editorial cartooning to Cal Alley was not the drawing of occasional outstanding works, but the constant demand of creating something publishable every day. He said that producing a cartoon required ten hours and twenty minutes—ten hours to think of an idea and twenty minutes to put it on paper. Since thinking of ideas was the most difficult part of his activity, he searched diligently for them. He regularly attended the newspaper's editorial meetings, read each issue of the paper completely and carefully, and listened to radio news reports as often as possible. Certain books, such as the *Bible, Uncle Remus*, and *Famous Quotations* also provided themes, although his use of Uncle Remus scenes declined over the years. Lewis Carroll's *Alice in Wonderland*, the plays of Shakespeare, and the characters in Charles Dickens' works also supplied sources for his use. Occasionally when an idea for a cartoon had been developed, he sat down and sketched rapidly until it was completed. He often made several drawings, from which he selected the one most clearly expressing his idea. Sometimes, however, after sketching for hours to be certain he was portraying the situation in the most effective way, he would return to the original idea of that day, feeling that he had examined all possibilities and therefore could be satisfied that he was giving best expression to the subject.

Cal Alley brought to his work an unusual dedication and persistence. The steady demands of the career required that he seek always for new themes and ideas and that he see everything in terms of how it could be placed on the drawing board. The current nature of his work required that most sketches be done on a day to day basis to insure their timeliness, although occasionally he was able to prepare a cartoon on a general topic to be used according to future need. His wife, Sissy, said later that "drawing was his whole life." Once when suffering from pneumonia he refused to be hospitalized so that he might remain at home to continue his drawing.

Recreational pursuits were necessarily adjusted to this arduous work schedule. Cal Alley had an interest in poker, which he played occasionally with friends, and golf, which he sometimes found time for at Galloway Park and Colonial Country Club. He also enjoyed swimming at the country club, but this sport too was one for which he could find only limited time. Even on holidays and vacations his time was never entirely free. His drawing materials were always taken with him on these occasions. Sometimes when he went out to dinner acquaintances would see him start sketching at the table when he had a new idea. It is probable that he often did not think of this activity as work. He did many drawings as gifts for friends and also guided his son, Rick, into developing his own cartooning talent.

Cal Alley's modesty and his personal view of his work probably prevented his giving much thought to the important position he occupied—that of leading cartoonist of a region occupying the lower Mississippi Valley between the newspaper trade areas of St. Louis and New Orleans. It is this significant position which gives Cal Alley's work value to historians of his part of the South. Historical writers usually consider newspapers to be a valid source of material for their studies because these papers reveal what the public thought at the time they were published. In all likelihood this assumption of the accuracy of newspaper records is made too uncritically by many historians, but it does seem to be correct in the case of Cal Alley's work.

Historians should, of course, be aware of the extent of a newspaper's readership. They also need to know whether the material in a newspaper agrees with the views of its readers. While it may be impossible to settle the question of whether editorial policy (cartoon or otherwise) reflects public opinion or creates it, most historians assume that there is a relationship between the beliefs of people and the policies of the newspapers they read.

Cal Alley's cartoons certainly reflected much of the public opinion of his city and region. They probably created some public opinion, too. Furthermore, by 1970 these cartoons were being circulated in 215,844 copies daily and 268,873 copies on Sundays. According to an estimate by the promotions department of the newspaper, each daily copy had more than two readers. It should not be assumed, though, that those who followed Cal Alley's work in *The Commercial Appeal* represented an average cross section of the area's population. It is likely that newspaper subscribers in any area are not typical of the general population. They tend to be more affluent and more highly educated. Cal Alley's audience, therefore, consisted mainly of middle and upper class citizens who, because of delivery arrangements of the newspaper, lived most often in Memphis and other smaller urban locations.

These readers represented the leadership class of Cal Alley's part of the South. By all indications the ideas that he expressed were generally those which were held by these people. The cartoonist's identification with this class was thorough and genuine. His political and economic views expressed in the newspaper were generally consistent with theirs throughout the entire quarter of a century before his death. Tennessee's reputation as "the Volunteer State" was one of its oldest traditions and Tennesseans, although their patriotism had sometimes involved much more talk than action, did take great pride in their support of the nation during its wars. Patriotism was also a dominant influence in the life of Cal Alley. One of his greatest disappointments was his failure, despite his best efforts and the influence of his friends, to get into military service during World War II. He suffered from an eye condition, nystagmus, which prevented his enlistment. His evaluation of national leaders was determined basically by the degree of patriotism he judged them to have.

Another way in which Cal Alley was associated with the leadership class of his area was in religious outlook. Since Memphis was located within an area known as "the Bible Belt," its leading citizens were expected to be supporters of religion. The work of *The Commercial Appeal*'s cartoonist was also consistently in support of the basic religious values of his area. Cal Alley held his personal religious views which were independent of the doctrine of any one church, but he had a deep respect for the religious views of members of all churches.

Cal Alley's identification with the established interests of the area naturally affected his drawing. Although cartoonists often achieve their greatest acclaim as critics of the status quo, the Memphis cartoonist was generally committed to its support. He did believe that cartoons were more effective when they were drawn to be against rather than for something, and this was practiced in his own sketches. But since his work was usually in support of the existing order, the caricatures which he drew were generally against people and movements which threatened its stability.

While Cal Alley directed some of his efforts toward reform topics (See Chapter V for examples), this was the exception to the general rule. It would certainly be an over-simplification to divide cartoonists into reformers and defenders of the status quo, but if such a division were made the Memphis artist would have to be included in the latter category. His work was basically that of a man who, despite some specific exceptions, approved of the society in which he lived. He deserves particular credit for presenting with such accuracy the prevailing views of his time and region. It is this true representation of the dominant public opinion of the Memphis area which gives these cartoons their historical value.

By 1970 Cal Alley had achieved notable success in his chosen profession. His position with a major regional newspaper was secure, and he had won many of the honors and awards available to a person in his profession. With increasing experience his artistic techniques had become more mature. His drawings became less filled with detail as he learned to convey more meaning with simpler lines. At the same time the variety of ideas and sources with which he illustrated his drawings had increased. His children had all grown up; and with no further responsibilities to draw the features "Hambone" and "The Ryatts," he was free to devote full time to the development of his editorial cartooning. At the age of fifty-four his greatest success seemed to be ahead of him.

It was during the summer of 1970 that his health began to fail. By the end of August he was in great pain. He had always been too busy to give much attention to illness on previous occasions, but this time his condition steadily became worse. On October 12, two days after his fifty-fifth birthday, he entered the hospital. The medical specialist who examined him diagnosed cancer of the lungs and spine and estimated that he probably could not live more than four to six weeks. The diagnosis was accurate. Cal Alley died on November 10, 1970.

CAL ALLEY

World War Two and the
Truman Administration

Calvin Lane Alley was 29 when he came to Memphis as editorial cartoonist for *The Commercial Appeal*. It was in the spring of 1945 and the most important news for readers was America's involvement in the Second World War. For more than three years after the surprise Japanese attack on Pearl Harbor on December 7, 1941, the energy of the United States had been directed almost without exception toward the prosecution of the war. This struggle, which involved the most formidable enemies ever faced by the nation, was viewed by Americans, and certainly by residents of the newspaper's trade area, as a stark conflict between good and evil.

In the opening days of May, soon after Cal Alley's arrival in Memphis, the newspaper carried the happiest news it had reported in several years. The exuberant headlines announced the collapse of the Third Reich and the consequent victory in Europe on what was designated as "V-E Day." The feeling of most Memphians was probably expressed by the celebrant in the editorial cartoon of May 8, who saw the occasion as one of festive joy.

The nation also, of course, celebrated the absolute defeat of the most dangerous of the three Axis nations. From the beginning the basic war strategy of the United States had been to allocate most of the American resources to the European theatre of operations while diverting a lesser amount to the Pacific to check the expansion of Japan until the war could be won in Europe. At V-E Day the first phase of this plan had succeeded. Italy and Germany, personified by cartoonists and doubtless by many citizens also in the form of their leaders, Mussolini and Hitler, were defeated unconditionally. The Cal Alley cartoon of June 12, 1945, was a drawing of the three Axis leaders—Hitler, Mussolini, and Hirohito, even though at this time the first two of these were dead. Mussolini had been summarily executed by anti-Fascist Italians, and Hitler had committed suicide in his Berlin bunker. However, the evidence of Hitler's death was obscured in the Russian occupation of shattered Berlin, and American newspapers had received only rumors of his fate.

America's celebration of V-E Day, though joyful, was restrained by the knowledge of the immense price that had been paid for the victory and by the prospect of the bitter struggle impending before Japan could be defeated. Scenes such as the one represented by the Cal Alley drawing of a small boy praying by his bed for his father who was absent in military service were found in many American homes as the nation mobilized the largest number of men ever gathered for any of its wars. Tennessee was to supply approximately ten percent of its population (315,501) for the armed forces. Casualties were increasing toward their maximum wartime total of 1,076,245 as the effects of the war were felt deeply in all states.

Developments during the summer months of 1945 brought the war to its conclusion in the Pacific. In July the Potsdam Conference was held by the three major allied leaders: Joseph Stalin, Winston Churchill, and Harry Truman, who had become president of the United States after the death of Franklin Roosevelt. Cal Alley's cartoon of July 18 depicted the Potsdam Conference being held in the background during the concluding phases of the American and British military suppression of Japan. The civilian leaders were drawn with their individual characteristics, while the military personnel were shown in their respective uniforms: America was represented by Uncle Sam wearing the uniform of a soldier; Britain became John Bull in the uniform of a British sailor; and Japan was depicted as a soldier with slant eyes, thick glasses and protruding teeth.

Russia's entry into the war against Japan, although late, was welcomed in the United States. Russia's participation was noted in the newspaper by a drawing of Stalin crushing Hirohito with a red hammer. This cartoon coincided with the general U. S. view at the time of Russia as a friend and ally.

The summer of 1945 also saw the event which may make the year one of the more significant in the history of mankind—the first successful application of atomic energy. So complete was the secrecy surrounding the Manhattan project that the news of the explosion of the atomic bomb at Hiroshima on August 6 came to the American people without warning. The initial experiments at the University of Chicago, the vast manufacturing project at Oak Ridge, Tennessee, and the first test explosion at Alamagordo, New Mexico, had been among the best kept secrets of the war. The great implications of the bombing of Hiroshima were slow to become apparent, but Cal Alley's cartoon of August 7 indicated both the immediate result and the long-term significance of the event. The new type of bomb, which was also dropped three days later on Nagasaki, was to bring a quick end to the Japanese refusal to surrender. The death's head depicted on the bomb falling on Japan symbolized the dread shadow of atomic destruction under which humanity was to live for decades, and which to some people would threaten the extinction of mankind on earth.

The conclusion of the war was an almost immediate result of the atomic bombing of Japan. Acceptable preliminary terms of surrender were agreed upon, generally along the lines of the allied policy of "unconditional surrender," and the American relief and joy at the winning of the nation's greatest war was expressed by the drawing of a happy Statue of Liberty on August 15. Within a week Lt. General Jonathan Wainright presided at the ceremony of surrender aboard the battleship *Missouri*, and the great war was over.

But the problems left by the war remained. One of the matters involving the most emotion was the question of punishment for those guilty of atrocities against civilians and of mistreatment of prisoners of war. This question was settled by the series of trials for war crimes and the punishment of most of those tried. The importance of the precedents established by these trials could only be determined in the future, but the opinion of the American people was that the penalties were well deserved.

Other problems were generated in the process of demobilization and conversion of the economy to a peacetime basis. As in previous wars, the American people were impatient with all delays in returning the armed forces to civilian life and in ending wartime economic controls. Although they had supported the war willingly when their country was attacked, their lack of a militaristic tradition and their ignorance of postwar foreign dangers led Americans into a headlong rush toward demobilization. Rationing and other economic controls were abandoned, military bases were closed, large quantities of material were declared surplus, and millions of men were quickly released to civilian life.

This national reconversion to civilian life was not always easy. The economy faltered under the strain as returning veterans faced inflation, labor turmoil, and shortages of housing and consumer goods.

One of the most noticeable postwar alterations was in education. Congress, by passing the G. I. Bill of Rights, gave financial aid to veterans for educational expenses. As a result of this act, perhaps one of the wisest ever enacted in the United States, changes were soon noticed on the campuses of colleges and universities across the nation. The prewar student body was changed by an influx of veterans, many of them older, more serious, and more mature than previous student groups. Many of them were married, and for the first time family housing became a feature of campuses, as barracks and quonset huts from unused military bases were converted to student use. These structures were to become characteristic of many institutions for more than two decades. The cartoon of September 2, 1947, included the characters found at institutions all across America in the years following the war.

To American expenses in the postwar years were added appeals from impoverished and devasted nations which had suffered during the war. The United States responded generously to these appeals, but doubts felt by individual Americans were expressed in the Columbus Day cartoon of 1945. This expenditure for foreign aid was to be one of the continuing expenses of the war. Also in 1945 one of Cal Alley's heroes, Gen. George Patton, died and was depicted with pistols and helmet entering Valhalla. After this year the Cal Alley cartoons were to deal with the issues of a civilian America in the postwar world.

The matter of civilian leadership in the years following the war was one which Cal Alley saw in sad contrast to the heroic heights of wartime. Harry Truman appeared as an inept bungler as he tried to continue the New Deal of Franklin Roosevelt, as a naive city boy lost in the woods while his liberal policies alienated the solid South, and as a blundering campaigner in the election of 1948. After his reelection he seemed to be unable to deal effectively with Congress and was able to salvage only the part of his legislative program that had the support of the faithful Southern conservatives.

The most alarming aspect of the Truman administration, and the one most mercilessly caricatured in the Alley cartoons, was the rapid increase in federal expenses. This deficit spending brought the nation to a fiscal condition which seemed to people of conservative economic views little better than that of America's destitute and importunate foreign friends. The closing years of the Truman administration were depicted as being characterized by scandals and corruption. The removal of the heroic General Douglas MacArthur was seen as the sort of action which might be expected from an administration represented by graft, fraud, and bribery involving deep-freezes and mink coats. By the close of the Truman era the public view of this situation was such that it was seen by Cal Alley as a handicap to the 1952 Democratic presidential candidate, Adlai Stevenson.

May 8, 1945

V-*E* DAY

June 17, 1945

Something For Daddy

WHO'D A-THOUGHT IT!

THE PUNY PUNK
IN THE TRIO,
AND HE'S STILL
ON HIS FEET

July 19, 1945

THE ENDLESS CHASE

July 18, 1945

SOME THINGS CAN'T WAIT

August 9, 1945

CONSIDERABLY SHORTENED

August 7, 1945

NO JAPAN

14

August 15, 1945

Oh, Happy Day!

WHAT BETTER WAY COULD THE SCORE BE SETTLED?

September 1, 1945

LET THE PUNISHMENT FIT THE CRIME

May 12, 1945

AT HOME AND ABROAD WITH THE G.I. SCORE CARD

November 18, 1945

Their Melancholy Days Are Come

September 2, 1947

BACK-TO-SCHOOLMATES

October 12, 1945

COLUMBUS DAY QUIZ

December 22, 1945

GOIN' HOME

February 28, 1946

MAYBE PLAIN DEALING IS MORE YOUR STYLE, HARRY

March 31, 1948

RECKON SOMEBODY OUGHTA TELL· 'IM?

June 17, 1948

THE FOOTSORE TRAVELER COMES LIMPING HOME

May 13, 1949

HARRY'S LEGISLATIVE CALENDAR

June 5, 1949

The 'Work Horse' He Could Do So Well Without

January 17, 1950

"BUDDHA-BUDDHA-BUDDHA"

FREE PILLS

FREE LUNCH

FREE PENSIONS

ALL PAY NO WORK

FREE SUBSIDIES

FREE ADVICE

WELFARE STATE

THE GULLIBLE

(23ᴿᴰ PSALM REVISED)

THE STATE IS MY SHEPHERD; I SHALL NOT WORK.
IT MAKETH ME TO LIE DOWN ON GOOD JOBS;
IT LEADETH ME BY THE STILL FACTORIES.

IT DEADENS MY SOUL; IT LEADETH ME IN
THE PATHS OF IDLENESS FOR POLITICS' SAKE.

YEA, THOUGH I WALK THROUGH THE VALLEY
OF SLOTHFULNESS AND ECONOMIC DISASTER,
I WILL FEAR NO EVIL, FOR IT WILL BE WITH ME;
ITS DOLE AND PATERNALISM, THEY COMFORT ME.

IT PREPARETH A UTOPIA FOR ME BY
APPROPRIATING THE EARNINGS OF THE FRUGAL;
IT FILLETH MY HEAD WITH FOOL
EXPECTATIONS, MY MOUNTING INEFFICIENKY
RUNNETH OVER.

SURELY GOODNESS AND MERCY SHALL
FOLLOW ME ALL THE DAYS OF MY LIFE;
I SHALL LIVE ON THE BOUNTY OF THE
STATE FOREVER.*

+R.H,

March 26, 1950

Life In A Juke Joint

November 13, 1951

Informal Visit

April 18, 1951

Adding Insult To Injury

October 30, 1952

The Real Plea

September 7, 1952

Discouraging, Isn't It?

The Cold War, Internal Subversion, and Korea

The happy dreams of the American people for tranquillity after World War II were not to be realized. Peace brought a disillusionment which was probably even more severe than that which had been experienced after World War I. At the close of the great crusade against the Axis powers, all of America's enemies were utterly defeated and there was no possible challenge to allied military power by any conceivable combination of nations; yet peace did not come and the security of the United States soon appeared to be in serious question.

The trouble was caused by a widening division among the victorious allied nations. Under the ruthless and astute leadership of Joseph Stalin, Russia rapidly extended both its boundaries and its iron control over the nations of eastern Europe. This aggressive expansion was seen by the Western allies as a direct threat to their security which must be checked. The alarm over this danger was sounded by Winston Churchill, who denounced the placing of an "iron curtain" across what was to have become a free and peaceful Europe, but the power of Great Britian had been drained by the exhausting effort of World War II. The only nation with sufficient power to face Russia was the United States, and it soon became apparent that if western Europe and the Mediterranean were to be held against Communism, the effort would have to come from America.

Thus the United States, though with considerable debate and some reluctance, became the leader of one of the two armed camps of nations in the world. The major arena for the struggle was Europe where money and arms from the west, as a part of the newly developed Marshall Plan, were committed to strengthen the shattered nations as a bulwark against Communism.

The situation which developed was perhaps not quite war, but it was certainly not peace. It soon came to be called "the cold war." Its battle sites included such places as Yugoslavia where the nationalist leader, Josip Tito, challenged Russian control, and Berlin where in 1948 Russia tried unsuccessfully to force the Western allies out of the city by blockade. By the close of the decade Uncle Sam seemed to Cal Alley and to many other Americans to be beleagured by militant Communism advancing on many fronts. Other alarming aspects of the cold war appeared. One of them was an arms race that included conventional and atomic weapons and culminated in the development of the hydrogen bomb, a weapon of such destructive power that the survival of civilization was placed in peril. Another product of the cold war was its enormous cost to the U. S. government. By the middle of the 1950's this expense had reached a total of forty-three billion dollars.

A public awareness of the expense and danger of the cold war during the 1950's led to diplomatic moves from the leaders of both sides toward a negotiation of disputes, but a basic lack of trust prevented substantial progress at any "summit" meetings.

By the close of the decade there were indications of some developments more favorable to the United States. Nikita Khrushchev's leadership of Russia seemed somewhat less of a threat to the west than that of Stalin's had been; and relations between the two major Communist powers, Russia and China, became increasingly strained. But America still had to face various incidents, some of which, like the loss of a U-2 spy plane over Russia, were both dangerous and embarrassing.

A weak United Nations filled with many new and impoverished states was not effectual in dealing with the confrontation of the two major power blocs, and the arms race accelerated through the 1960's. The American people had learned by this time to live in a state in which peace and security could not be assured and in which all mankind lived under the shadow of nuclear disaster. To Cal Alley the most alarming danger, and the one to which he devoted frequent warnings, was his nation's apathy in the face of the threat of Communism.

But dangers from without were not the only ones faced by the United States. During the early years of the confrontation with Communism, it became evident that Russia had organized networks of spies in America. Some of these had been extraordinarily effective, particularly in the theft of atomic secrets. The shock of this successful penetration of the United States by enemy agents spread until many Americans who had been associated in earlier times with the Communist party came under investigation. These people, some of them in high positions in Hollywood and in the government, were seen by the Memphis cartoonist as dangerous enemies of the nation who took advantage of American freedom to seek protection behind the U. S. constitution when in reality they deserved to be punished by death if they were spies or by unemployment if they were Communist sympathizers. A classic case of this era was that of Alger Hiss, about whose conviction in 1950 Cal Alley expressed what was probably the view of the majority of Americans. His views about Communist sympathizers of all kinds were forthright and he had little patience with those who took less than an adamant stand against Communism.

A new phase in the cold war began abruptly in June, 1950, when the United States became involved in armed hostilities in Korea. The fragile peace based on a partition of that nation into two zones, one controlled by the U. S. and the other by Russia and China, was broken by the armed invasion across the thirty-eighth parallel by Communist forces from the north.

The United States, taking advantage of the temporary absence of Russia from the United Nations, was able to secure the approval of the international body for armed resistance to North Korean aggression. The substance of this resistance was supplied by the United States, with token forces being sent by other nations which were among America's allies in the United Nations. Since the other nations together supplied less than ten percent of the military forces, the war to defend South Korea was in reality an American war; and the nation quickly rushed naval, land, and air units to the peninsula. As casualties and costs increased, the American people soon found themselves engaged again in a major military effort. This was to all intents and purposes a war, but it was unlike any war the nation had experienced before. Command was exercised, at least nominally, not by the United States but by the United Nations, and the conduct of the war was determined by considerations that were but little understood by the public.

The initial American intervention came just in time to prevent the complete defeat of South Korea, but by the autumn of 1950 the United Nations had landed sufficient forces at Pusan to drive the North Korean armies back and to launch an amphibious invasion at Inchon. By mid-winter, the north was almost completely overrun.

For diplomatic reasons General Douglas MacArthur was restrained from driving north of the Manchurian border, and a counterattack by hordes of Communist Chinese "volunteers" crossed the Yalu River and changed the direction of United Nations movement to a precipitate retreat toward the South. Despite winter weather and in the face of overwhelming numerical odds, a heroic American effort did succeed in evacuating most military personnel who had been cut off by the onrushing Communist attack. The retreat was eventually checked and by the spring of 1951 a new battle line had been stabilized near the thirty-eighth parallel.

For the next two years the situation was one of intense frustration for Cal Alley, as he experienced the confusion and disappointment felt by many of the American people. By all indications the nation was at war. Casualties increased beyond the totals of the War of 1812, the Mexican War, and the Spanish-American War, while the home-front was characterized by hoarding, inflation, and the draft. Yet the public was told that what was happening in Korea was not a war; it was merely a police action. And the full use of military power, including atomic weapons, was not allowed. A nation accustomed to winning its wars was ordered by its own government to fight without winning. To avoid starting a third World War, which might have brought mutual annihilation to the major powers, the fighting in Korea was deliberately limited in its objectives. This military stalemate did not end until 1953 when negotiations which had started in 1951 led to eventual settlement. The Memphis cartoonist, however, joined many of his countrymen in the conviction that Communist China, as a consequence of its opposition to the United States in Korea, should be barred permanently from membership in the United Nations.

March 4, 1947

KING CANUTE MAKES A CLEAN SWEEP OF IT

February 25, 1948

ACCORDING TO THE BOOK

May 13, 1948

ECHO FROM MUNICH

July 2, 1948

THEY CERTAINLY SOUND CONVINCING

December 2, 1948

THE SPLIT

December 7, 1948

REMEMBER PEARL HARBOR

ONCE UPON A TIME, THERE WAS AN ARAB—

July 24, 1949

First, Be Sure He Can Handle A Bazooka

Creeping, Crawling War Of Nerves

February 17, 1955

We Can Hope

May 9, 1956

Dig 43 Billion And What Do You Get?

March 4, 1958

Mountains Out Of Mole Hills

April 1, 1958

Look Out For Back-Slappers

August 18, 1960

Over OUR Territory

September 18, 1960

No. 1 Boy, Him Clumsy

December 26, 1961

'Twas The Day After Christmas—

January 14, 1962

Two Diggers—One Headstone

September 21, 1967

Roll Call In The UN

December 11, 1968

History's Most Senseless "Race"

June 23, 1959

Pit And Pendulum

September 3, 1961

Under Threatening Skies

March 1, 1964

For The Love Of God, Wake Up!

September 25, 1963

Reporting For Duty, Sir!

May 10, 1960

Caught!

February 22, 1952

The Meat Of It

January 25, 1955

No Room For Doubt

August 11, 1967

A Look At Our World

September 24, 1969

Quite A $onic Boom!

December 16, 1949

AT PRESENT, THE SITUATION ISN'T QUITE CLEAR

October 22, 1947

MAKE-UP ARTIST

October 28, 1947

A SANCTUARY TURNED INTO A RATHOLE

January 27, 1950

IN A RUT

June 16, 1949

YOU FIGURE IT OUT—WE CAN'T

April 6, 1951

No Place For Maudlin Sympathy

October 16, 1953

"Would You Rather Answer To Me?"

October 25, 1963

Cold (Cash) War

July 25, 1950

THE MORALE BUILDERS

November 22, 1950

SOUTHBOUND TRAFFIC ONLY?

December 27, 1950

THEY'VE DONE THE IMPOSSIBLE

March 29, 1951

Charlie MacArthur

April 25, 1951

Our Only Forward Movement In Korea

September 23, 1951

Time To Resume 'Talk' On Our Terms

October 7, 1951

Heartbreak Ridge, U.S.A.

May 17, 1953

Battle Cries!

The Heck Of It Is, You Never Know

July 6, 1954

"Over My Dead Body!"

The Eisenhower Decade

Cal Alley shared the admiration of the American people for General Dwight D. Eisenhower, and participated also in their anticipation as to what part the famous war hero might play in the nation's political leadership, if it could be determined what party the general belonged to and what his ambitions might be. Mr. Alley had developed a deep respect for the conservative principles he associated with the Republican party and saw in it a remedy for the liberalism of the New Deal and the Fair Deal which he had opposed for many years. Having observed the defeatism and the inaction of many Republican party regulars, particularly in the South, he sympathized with the reforming moderates in the party rather than with the Old Guard. A strong two-party system was long overdue in the South, he felt; and a revived, more broadly-based Republican party was badly needed by the nation.

Accordingly, the Memphis cartoonist was pleased with the successful maneuvers of the newer, reform-minded members of the Grand Old Party in the nominating convention of 1952. Even more, he was gratified by the nomination of Dwight Eisenhower and the consequent defeat of Senator Robert Taft of Ohio, who had been the champion of the party's Old Guard. The Eisenhower selection by the Republicans was the action required to end a twenty-year period of defeat for their party.

To Cal Alley, Eisenhower's defeat of the Democratic candidate, Governor Adlai Stevenson, in the presidential election restored dignity and a proper sense of direction to American government. Despite this approval the new president and members of his party were not above close and critical examination by the Memphis caricaturist. One of the Republican members of this Congress who attracted most public attention was Senator Joseph McCarthy of Wisconsin, who made vituperative charges of widespread Communist infiltration of the government. Although President Eisenhower was careful to avoid an open break with McCarthy, Cal Alley did not hesitate to depict the controversial senator as incompetent and irresponsible. Alley's political sympathies during the Eisenhower Era were consistently against the extreme right wing elements of the Republican party.

During President Eisenhower's first term in office the press exposed a plan by the government to approve the building of a mammoth electrical generating plant near Memphis. This steam plant, to be constructed by the Dixon-Yates syndicate, would operate in competition with the Tennessee Valley Authority, and would be a major gain for private power interests which had been opposed to TVA throughout the Roosevelt and Truman administrations. Newspapers in Tennessee and the other states in the TVA service area had developed a tradition of support for the agency, and could usually be counted on to come to its aid. These newspapers, including *The Commercial Appeal*, joined in the defense of the Tennessee Valley Authority. Alley caricatured the Republican administration for its support of the Dixon-Yates plan by showing this scheme as a collusion of big business and government which might be comparable with the Teapot Dome scandal of the Warren Harding administration. Needless to say, the plan was detrimental to the popularity of the G. O. P. in the TVA area. So effective and so unrelenting were the attacks on the Dixon-Yates arrangement that the Eisenhower administration, finally concluding that the power plan was a mistake, accepted a compromise plan offered by the mayor of Memphis and abandoned Dixon-Yates.

In the presidential election of 1956, however, *The Commercial Appeal* and its editorial cartoonist gave willing support to President Eisenhower's campaign for a second term. Adlai Stevenson, who was nominated a second time as the Democratic candidate, was shown as a leader lacking in the firmness and strength needed to guide the nation through crises in foreign relations that were likely to come as a result of the cold war. Nor were the other possible leaders of the Democratic party (G. Mennen Williams, Hubert Humphrey, Harry Truman, Averill Harriman, and Estes Kefauver) seen as offering acceptable alternatives for national leadership. The reelection of Dwight Eisenhower was a welcome outcome to Cal Alley, who continued to give support to the President throughout his second term. Some incidents, though, such as the scandal involving presidential staff chief Sherman Adams and industrialist Bernard Goldfine—the "vicuna coat" scandal—were lampooned in the Memphis newspaper. Despite his occasional critical drawings, Cal Alley considered Eisenhower to be one of his favorite presidents. He found him to be a pleasant contrast to the Fair Deal president who preceded him and the New Frontier one who followed him.

November 4, 1951

Ladies-In-Waiting

February 1, 1952

Needle Shy

March 14, 1952

What's That About An Elephant's Memory?

July 3, 1952

The Dilemma Of The Whatsit

July 11, 1952

Must've Run Over Something Mighty Sharp

December 3, 1953

Good Old-Fashioned Discipline

May 27, 1954

Battling Joe

October 19, 1954

Don't SAY That!

October 29, 1954

Aw, Ike! Cut Out The Monkeyshines

June 29, 1955

Steam Generating Plant

November 29, 1955

Moderation, Adlai? You're In The Wrong Crowd

November 2, 1956

"Now Here's What I'd Do - - - Hey - - - Fellas!?"

September 24, 1958

What He Left The Girl Behind Him

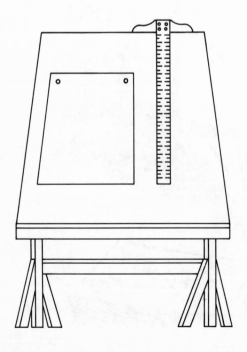

Labor, Crime, and the Supreme Court

During the quarter of a century following the close of World War II, several issues out of the nation's past assumed a new and sharply controversial importance. Three of these about which Cal Alley was most concerned and on which he held most firm and consistent positions were labor, the Supreme Court and crime.

Organized labor was in an advantageous position at the end of the war. Aided by favorable governmental action during the New Deal and further strengthened by its record of loyal support for the war effort, labor entered the peacetime era with unprecedented influence and with great political power. As the nation's economy started an extended period of growth and inflation, union leaders determined to hold the gains they had made and also to improve their relative economic position. These aims were, of course, contrary to those of management and as a result of this clash of interests America entered a protracted era of labor strife.

Although the battles and skirmishes in this economic conflict were sometimes won by management, organized labor generally made significant gains. Strikes usually resulted in at least a part of the increase initially sought, and regular raises were often secured by bargaining without resorting to a strike. This success of the labor unions was matched by a growth of their political power as their financial resources, votes, and organization became an indispensable bulwark of the Democratic party. Within a decade after the war, organized labor was probably as important to the Democratic party as big business had traditionally been to the Republican party.

A political and economic development of this magnitude was certain to produce varying viewpoints. The rise to power of labor unions was especially alarming to conservatives, Southerners, supporters of management, and adherents of the Republican party. As a person included in all of these categories, Cal Alley adopted a firm and predictable position toward the aspirations and activities of organized labor. He saw the status of American workers, which was characterized by a relatively high standard of living, as being an enviable one which should be accepted with gratitude rather than being changed by unions and strikes. As a cartoonist he personified the labor unions in caricatures of their leaders, the most prominent of them all being pilloried by his pencil. John L. Lewis, Philip Murray, Harry Bridges, David Beck, James Hoffa, and Walter Reuther were labor leaders depicted in varying degrees of disfavor.

Another source of power and of disturbing change in America aroused similar feelings beginning during the 1950's. It was the United States Supreme Court which, ironically enough, under the direction of Republican Chief Justice Earl Warren, began a series of decisions rendering new interpretations of the United States constitution. The court had been embroiled in controversy as early as the tenure of Chief Justice John Marshall, but the Warren court soon became involved in an unusual degree of acrimony. The most controversial, and possibly the most epochal, of its actions was the decision of May, 1954, ruling segregated education unconstitutional in public institutions. Other decisions, such as those limiting mandatory prayer in public education and those extending the rights of persons accused of crimes, occasioned considerable criticism, although less than the desegregation ruling.

The United States Supreme Court became the most criticized part of American government among white, conservative Southerners in particular, and among conservatives in general. The Cal Alley cartoons showed the court, represented by Earl Warren in judicial robes, as having usurped powers properly belonging to Congress and as being influenced by black, minority pressure groups to act against the true interests of the people. Earl Warren's threat to the traditional structure of American government was compared, perhaps facetiously, although many readers of *The Commercial Appeal* certainly agreed with the comparison, with the danger from the Russian government. The court continued to receive criticism until 1969 when the new Republican administration of President Richard Nixon gave hope for the appointment of more conservative judges to the tribunal.

A related issue which was a source of continuing alarm to the Memphis cartoonist, as it was to many other citizens, was the rise of crime in America. Although improved reporting of crime statistics may have been responsible for some of the increase, the figures still were disturbing and the seriousness of the development was unquestionable. The percentages of major offenses increased year after year while the court system, it seemed to some Americans, instead of dealing firmly with lawbreakers, actually hampered the police in their efforts to control crime. Many aspects of this complex problem occupied the attention of Cal Alley. He was concerned about the immediate causes of crime, including the influence on children of literature and television which dealt with topics of sex and crime. His cartoons gave attention also to an increasingly bothersome feature of lawlessness which received much notice during the fifties under the descriptive label "juvenile delinquency."

During the decade of the sixties, new aspects of crime came to the attention of the public and were included as subjects for cartoons in the Memphis newspaper. Criticism was directed at the tendency of the penal and judicial system to allow criminal offenders to remain free through bond, appeal, and parole, where they were often guilty of other offenses. Another development of the 1960's was the appearance of large-scale riots in American cities. These disturbances, occurring mainly in black urban areas, were particularly alarming to those already concerned about crime. Riots were highly visible, extremely destructive to property, and given much attention by news media. Police departments proved to be badly prepared to deal with public disorders and their attempts to control rioters often led to charges that officers were guilty of brutality. Another pattern in the nation's crime involved a vast increase in violations of narcotics laws. From the small, though serious, problem depicted in the cartoon of June 28, 1951, the drug problem expanded greatly during the next nineteen years. By the time Cal Alley drew his last cartoon dealing with the subject a large percentage of American youth was using illegal drugs.

While younger people tended to view narcotics offenses tolerantly and sometimes even approvingly, as violations of the prohibition laws had been viewed during the 1920's, most older Americans found nothing about them acceptable. This view was expressed firmly by the Cal Alley cartoons. Perhaps his greatest concern about crime, though, was with the complacency of American citizens in the face of a great and growing problem that he felt endangered the survival of the nation. The cartoon of March 20, 1960, entitled "Pompeii, 1960 A. D.," was especially illustrative of this belief.

September 3, 1950

Bringing Home The Bacon

January 18, 1946

SOLUTION NO. 99½ FOR A QUICK END TO STRIKES

October 30, 1949

The 'Trick Or Treat' Racket

April 24, 1959

"I'd Like To Help You, Son --- BUT ---

May 13, 1965

Tollgate Labor

May 8, 1946

ON THE FIRST ANNIVERSARY OF A GLORIOUS VICTORY

September 8, 1948

'I WAS NAKED AND YE CLOTHED ME - - -'

May 21, 1957

He Ain't Felt Nothin', Yet!

September 24, 1957

Drop 'Im!

January 31, 1958

Hasn't He Heard?

September 30, 1958

'You're Too Late, Comrade'

August 28, 1958

Oyez! Oyez! The Supreme Court Is Now In Session

May 28, 1963

The White Man's Burden

June 5, 1968

"Nobody Gave ME A Second Chance"

October 19, 1958

Benched

June 24, 1965

Madame Defarge

May 23, 1969

Fashion Note:
Skirts May Be Longer Soon

March 20, 1960

Pompeii, 1960 A.D.

November 15, 1953

The Baby Sitters

May 3, 1955

On His Way Up

November 9, 1958

"Hey, Mister . . . Got A Minute?"

January 17, 1960

Stone Walls Do Not A Prison Make

December 9, 1962

"I . . . have spoken!"

May 18, 1965

Let There Be No Doubt!

October 3, 1965

Disabled

June 28, 1951

Feeding Ground

June 10, 1970

Blame The Piper . . . Not The Kids

Education, the Economy, Space, and Reform

In the public social and political issues which develop during his career, a newspaper cartoonist finds both opportunity and hazard. On one hand they provide the material for his livelihood; on the other, they expose his personal views on controversial matters to the most exacting public scrutiny. It would not be surprising if cartoonists should occasionally have doubts about exposing their positions on some questions about which people hold particularly strong emotional views, preferring instead to deal with more neutral topics. If Cal Alley was ever tempted to restrain the expression of any convictions, his cartoons give no indication of it. His views generally corresponded to those of the management and readers of *The Commercial Appeal*, but they were always stated clearly and without equivocation. His positions were well illustrated, for example, on the subjects of the economy, education, reform, and on the competitive development of space exploration by Russia and the United States.

The quarter of a century when the Cal Alley cartoons were being drawn was marked by a continuing change in the economy. While there were some fluctuations, usually involving short periods of recession, the general course of the economy was one of steady growth and inflation. The worst fears of those who lived through the 1930's were not realized. A depression did not come after either World War II or the Korean War. But the lack of stability in the economy was a source of concern to Americans who had such fears. The economy never achieved a static position. Inflation continued year after year; the gross national product increased steadily; and federal budgets moved regularly upward. This continuing expansion of the economy brought an improved economic position to most citizens, but it produced discontent in two ways. On one hand some people lost relative financial position or were left even further behind in the increasing affluence. On the other hand the general prosperity was received by many with a sense of suspicion and dread. Remembering the decade-long upsurge in the economy before the great crash of 1929, they feared that the growth could not last.

To those whose economic views were rooted in the classical economic theory of *laissez faire*, such as Cal Ally, it seemed that fundamental economic laws were being broken and that this violation invited serious trouble. The cartoonist viewed inflation as an evil, and his work throughout the entire period gives evidence of this view.

The size of federal budgets was another source of concern. In 1949, the Truman budget of $41,000,000,000 seemed inordinately high. From that time until the appearance of his cartoon of January 25, 1967, on the Johnson budget of $135,000,000,000—more than three times the size of the one in 1949—Cal Alley persistently scored successive budget increases. The cartoonist's warnings that increasing deficit spending could not go on indefinitely were obviously not accepted by leaders in the federal government, for the budgets continued to increase and the national debt to grow during the administrations of all U. S. presidents of both parties.

Other cartoons dealt with the confusion of the American people, represented by the cartoon figure "John Q. Public," in the face of increasing taxes, rising prices, and an economy that seemed to be out of control. Some of the drawings revealed a concept of individuals being caught between powerful organized forces, both industrial and labor. The most fundamental concern about the economic developments in the nation, though, was that the source of the trouble was the failure of individuals to exercise sufficient restraint in seeking their own advantage.

Another change that presented new challenge and opportunity to cartoonists during the cold war era was the sudden appearance of space technology with its extensive implications for national prestige and military power. It had been generally known for several years that both the United States and Russia were experimenting with the development of rockets, both nations having captured and used personnel and technology from the Nazi rocket program. But the Russian launching during October, 1957, of Sputnik, the first earth satellite, had great impact on world opinion. Following only a few months after their first successful firing of an intercontinental ballistic missile, Sputnik was exploited masterfully by Russian propaganda.

While a large part of the world's press was critical of America's lack of success, Cal Alley remained confident that the nation's initiative would overcome the Russian lead. Even though he depicted the repeated failures of the American rocket program during the years of Russian progress toward the first successful orbiting of a man—cosmonaut Yuri Gargarin—in space, Cal Alley remained confident that his nation's initiative would eventually overcome the Russian lead. His confidence was justified when America's first astronaut, John Glenn, was launched into orbit in 1962. The American space program gradually became competitive with that of the Soviet Union. By the time of the first moon landing in 1969, American scientific and industrial activity, stimulated by sums of money greater than those used to develop the atomic bomb, had overcome the

Russian lead and placed the United States in a position of obvious superiority.

During the decades of the 1940's through the 1960's, another source of change appeared in education, which had traditionally been one of the more stable parts of society. The Memphis cartoonist held a deep respect for the value of education in general. His work gives indication of this feeling, although he felt free to deal critically with any specific aspects of education. While his drawings reminded the young of the necessity of attending school, he was disturbed by the problems of rapid expansion in higher education. In 1955 he suggested limiting enrollment by the adoption of higher admission requirements. An equally alarming development in the schools was their mediocre quality which failed to challenge the most talented students. This was condemned in a cartoon of April 3, 1960, and in an accompanying newspaper editorial entitled "Escaping the 'Cult of Mediocrity.'" Although Cal Alley recognized that education was severely limited by a lack of money, he was always prevented from supporting fundamental reforms by his steadfast conviction that financial aid for schools should only come from local sources.

An examination of the complete series of Cal Alley cartoons gives evidence of a person who was generally pleased with the society in which he lived and who directed most of his criticism at those who threatened to change it. His basic support of the status quo (noted elsewhere in this book) was one of the most noticeable characteristics of all of his work. The decades during which he worked for *The Commercial Appeal*, however, were times when various ideas for reform appeared. Cal Alley gave support to some of them. One reform for which he campaigned at a surprisingly early date was that of protecting the ecological balance of the American environment. The first of his drawings on this theme appeared on Columbus Day, 1952. Shortly before his death in 1970, he was still sounding this alarm.

He also supported those reforms which called for changes in the military draft, the electoral college, and the welfare system. But he did not approve all reform ideas. For example, when demands were made to lower the voting age from 21 to 18 years, he protested the proposed change. The generally conservative nature of his work is evident throughout his entire career.

April 27, 1948

A SAD ENTRY

November 21, 1948

Now You Sees 'Em, Now You Don't

May 27, 1970

Affluent America

May 9, 1957

Ungrateful Little Spendthrift!

November 13, 1949

Everybody Just Goes Along For The Ride

January 7, 1949

THE RELUCTANT '49er

January 25, 1967

The One And Only Certain Thing About It

YOUR CONGRESS AT WORK

April 8, 1966

Just What We Need .. Rain In A Flood

We May Have To 'Give In' A Little, Says The Government

January 15, 1958

Move Over!

January 16, 1958

For Cryin' Out Loud, We Still Have The Cow

August 10, 1958

We Know A Few Tricks, Too

January 14, 1960

All We Can Do Is "Rare Back" And Watch

February 12, 1960

Two More Animals Russia Has Launched

November 5, 1967

Feet Of Clay

July 21, 1969

New Glory For Old Glory

September 15, 1954

Our Teachers—Greatest Bargain Since Manhattan

September 4, 1945

March 25, 1955

A Suggested Entrance "Fee"

April 3, 1960

Forced To Follow The Leader

March 2, 1958

Lassie, Come Home!

October 12, 1952

If Columbus Had Arrived Today

May 1, 1970

Anybody Listenin'?

March 5, 1967

Misery's Got Company

July 12, 1968

No, This Isn't The Republican Convention

IT'S THE BIGGER TRUCKS LOBBY!

March 19, 1954

He Doesn't Understand—It's Time We Did

July 9, 1961

Wearing Mighty Thin

July 28, 1959

Bermudas Just Aren't Our Style

Some People Don't Know Which End's Up

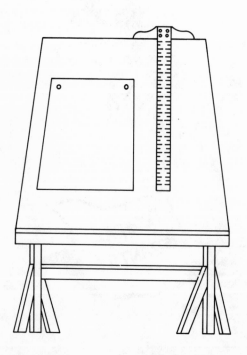

Local Issues

When Cal Alley arrived in Memphis in 1945 the most obvious factor in local politics, both to city residents and to outsiders, was that the city was dominated by Edward Hull "Boss" Crump. After his migration to Memphis from Mississippi in 1893, Mr. Crump had built a political machine more powerful and efficient than any seen in the state since William Blount had bossed the Tennessee area more than a century earlier. The Crump machine exercised iron control over Shelby County, generally directed the votes of a number of adjoining counties, and by delivering totalitarian size majorities in these counties was usually able to dictate the choice of candidates in state-wide elections. Since Shelby County alone contained almost one-fifth of the votes in Tennessee, a state in which elections were traditionally evenly balanced, the Crump endorsement usually guaranteed victory. The machine was in firm control of the city of Memphis in the mid-forties and was not effectively challenged until Estes Kefauver's campaign for the U. S. Senate in 1948. Such was the power of the Crump organization that state candidates opposed by it were sometimes afraid to come to Memphis; and when they did appear, troublesome incidents had a way of occurring to harrass them. Boss Crump exercised so much power and influence that Memphis was more nearly personified by him than by any other person.

Despite the importance of Mr. E. H. Crump, Cal Alley did not attempt to portray him until after a year of working for *The Commercial Appeal*. When the Crump cartoons did begin to appear, however, they were outstanding examples of the art. The political leader's most noticeable features—his glasses, heavy eyebrows, and thatch of white hair—were emphasized, yet the drawings had a remarkable resemblance to Mr. Crump himself. Another artistic technique appeared when with skillful strokes of the pencil the cartoonist transformed Boss Crump into Bossy the Cow. This characterization continued, and throughout the era the powerful political boss appeared regularly in the newspaper as a gentle domestic animal. Although relations between the political boss and the cartoonist were on a friendly basis personally, Cal Alley considered his role to be that of critic and further considered it to be a normal state of affairs that a politician would oppose restriction imposed on him by a critical press. The cartoons continued to be critical, but they were characterized by wry irony rather than by personal bitterness.

Perhaps Cal Alley was restrained from a more direct attack on Boss Crump, like the savage caricature of New York Boss William Tweed by cartoonist Thomas Nast, by his belief that the principal issue in Memphis politics was a struggle between those in office and those outside who wanted in. It was thus impossible to see the Crump machine as altogether wrong and those who crusaded against it as completely selfless. The drawings in the Memphis newspaper took caustic note of Mr. Crump's obstruction of the Edward Ward Carmack campaign in 1946, of his quarrels with Mayor Watkins Overton, and of his obstructive tactics concerning the opening of the new bridge and the financing of the city bus system. By the fifties his insistence on a low tax rate for Memphis had caused a patchwork of problems as the city continued to grow without having adequate financial resources. Mr. Crump was pictured as being responsible for these difficulties, but the subordinate politicians in the city—such as Claude Armour, Joe Boyle, E. W. Hale, and Frank Tobey—fared even less well. In the cartoons, they were drawn as lesser figures in comparison with the boss himself. When Mr. Crump died in October, 1954, his obituary cartoon marked the close of an era.

With the death of E. H. Crump, Memphis passed out of a period of strong government and entered a time characterized by political confusion and lack of leadership. Like many other powerful leaders, he had failed to arrange for a successor to replace him; and his followers, having lived in his heavy shadow, proved unable to rule as he had. Mr. Crump's opponents as well as his supporters agreed that Memphis political life was much less interesting without him.

This decline of interest in Memphis politics was reflected in Cal Alley's work. Local political developments were given less attention in his drawings until the mid-1960's, when the continuing crises of Memphis leadership resulted in a movement to discard the city's old commission form of government and replace it with a city council. It had been obvious, even before the death of Boss Crump, that the commission functioned effectively only because its members followed coherent orders from the boss and did not have freedom to pursue separate policies. Left without central leadership, the various holders of commission offices spent more than a decade in feudal squabbling until the Program of Progress, which included the new city council, was approved by popular vote in 1967. The adoption of this new city charter had the enthusiastic support of *The Commercial Appeal*. The newspaper's cartoons were a part of this support. In the person of incumbent Mayor William Ingram, who opposed the Program of Progress, Cal Alley found the best subject for political caricature since E. H. Crump.

The cartoons of Cal Alley which dealt with topics concerning his own city were characterized by two rather contradictory themes. On one hand, he had a deep pride in, and respect for, his hometown. But at the same time he experienced frustration and disappointment with what he considered to be backwardness and a failure of leadership that allowed many opportunities for progress to be lost. The progressive accomplishments of the city—such as the completion of the new bridge in 1949, the chartering of Memphis State University in 1957, and the completion of the municipal stadium in 1965—were all noted in his cartoons, as was the city's pride in singer Elvis Presley.

But the drawings also chronicled a long list of inadequacies, including the persistence of Sunday blue laws; the long overdue demise of prohibition; the filth allowed in Memphis slums and McKellar Lake; the lack of attention to the municipal zoo; the slowness of the city in completing the annexation of adjacent areas; the wanton destruction of the city's historical heritage; the refusals to proceed with expressway and airport construction; the political maneuvering involved in the decision to build a municipal power plant; the resistance to flouridation of the city water supply; and the obscurantism of the Memphis censor, Lloyd Binford, which limited the citizens' entertainment to the censor's own antiquated and restricted views.

With such a background of difficulties, the efforts of Martin Luther King to aid the black sanitation workers of the city was seen as just another problem. One of the causes of Memphis' difficulties was the low tax rate, and in Cal Alley's opinion solutions could only be achieved if the city voters would make the difficult and unlikely decision to increase local taxes. Even after the racial turmoil of 1968, he continued to be confident that the joint black and white leadership of the city could make progress together. This belief was expressed in his unpublished cartoon dated September 27, 1970.

September 6, 1946

IT'S PLUMB NATCHUL TO WANTA ROAM FREE

March 24, 1946

It's An Opportunity, Folks!

July 11, 1946

THAT NIGHT TRAIN TO MEMPHIS

April 3, 1951

Here's That Bossy Again

November 29, 1949

HORATIUS, JR.

February 9, 1951

What? AGAIN?

March 28, 1952

At Least, They're Looking

March 25, 1954

Another Patch In The Quilt

August 2, 1950

PRINCIPAL ISSUE

October 17, 1954

February 8, 1953

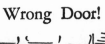

June 29, 1966

All Systems A-OK!

July 17, 1966

Immobile Object And Irresistible Force

October 20, 1966

Forever Blowing Bubbles

September 24, 1967

Above The Crowd

November 3, 1967

"Thanks For Delivering, Doc"

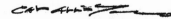

October 16, 1959

Memphis Looks "Ahead"

April 30, 1946

A MATTER OF PRIDE AND GOOD SENSE

October 16, 1949

There's A Great Day Comin'

January 9, 1957

He's Earned His Stripes

October 3, 1963

What Used To Be Mary's Little Lamb

IT FOLLOWS HER TO SCHOOL **EACH** DAY

December 31, 1965

Three Big Entries In A Finished Diary

January 18, 1966

"By Golly, This Thing's Fascinating!"

December 18, 1969

The Fuzz

August 15, 1967

Swallowing A Camel And Choking On A Gnat

February 8, 1955

To Your Health!

June 28, 1967

Another "Wolf" At Our Door

April 15, 1966

Formerly Known As "Bluff City"

April 4, 1965

The Timid Eagle

April 28, 1964

Mister, Let's See Your Driver's License

September 10, 1959

"Them Things Sho' Move, Don't They!"

December 1, 1954

Maybe The Best Way Out

September 19, 1957

Tree Jumped Out And Hit A Car Again

December 23, 1952

Hope Springs Eternal

April 9, 1952

Something To Read While You Wait

February 20, 1946

WHAT SHOOTIN', MR. BINFORD?

October 26, 1965

Right On Cue

February 16, 1968

Garbage!!

March 22, 1968

A Case Of Grab It Or Drown

September 27, 1970 [not published]

WE'VE NEARLY GOT IT MADE ... LET'S GO!

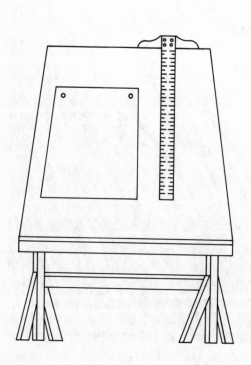

The South and Tennessee in Transition

One of the most important influences on the editorial cartooning of Cal Alley was the fact that he was a native Southerner who spent his life in a particularly unreconstructed part of the South. West Tennessee, long noted for its conservatism, had much more in common with Mississippi and other parts of the deep South than it did with the eastern part of the same state. It is impossible to understand the viewpoint of the Cal Alley drawings without realizing that they expressed a very strong regional outlook. National and international developments were all seen from this vantage point, but it was expressed most strongly in the cartoons dealing with the South itself. These drawings, representing a visual record of many concepts characteristic of the region, show the section as it was seen by many Southerners, especially in the circulation area of *The Commercial Appeal*.

It was the fate of Cal Alley to be born in a society probably more stable and traditional than any in the United States, yet to spend his adult life in a time when the South was forced to undergo changes more drastic than any experienced since the Civil War and Reconstruction almost a century earlier. One source of change in the section was its growing industrialization which brought not only increased wealth but also labor strife, unions, depletion of natural resources, and outside control of more of the Southern economy. All of these were upsetting to the area's previously closed social and economic structures, but the greatest force for change was the vigorously expressed disapproval of the remainder of the United States. The focus of these attacks was the South's treatment of the Negro, and the criticism hurt because it was both true and hypocritical. Blacks in the South did of course experience systematic, widespread, and unfair discrimination. Deliberately segregated in almost all activities, they were denied many rights enjoyed by whites. But the record of the rest of the country was far from perfect, and it seemed to many white Southerners that outsiders were more interested in criticizing the South than in dealing with their own injustices.

These attacks from outsiders caused many Southern people to react by becoming increasingly defensive about their section and by viewing it, particularly its past, as an ideal society in a golden age. Both of these themes appear in the drawings about the South, which emphasized the superiority of the Southern way of life and called attention to the unsolved problems of the North. Cal Alley's southernism, which was manifest in his drawings, still represented a more moderate view than that of many defenders of the section. Consistently opposed, as was his newspaper, to the Ku Klux Klan's use of force and terror, he felt that incidents of violence only played into the hands of the South's enemies. Like many other Southerners before him, Cal Alley hoped to find a sectional defense in the doctrine of state sovereignty; and like them, he found disappointingly little support for this doctrine on the part of other states.

Northern criticism and Southern defense was an old story, but more radical changes were in store for the South during the 1950's. On May 17, 1954, the U. S. Supreme Court, in one of its more significant decisions, declared racial segregation in public education to be unconstitutional. To blacks and their supporters it was a long overdue guarantee of their basic rights and a welcome opportunity to participate more fully in the American dream. To conservative white Southerners, though, it was a particularly heinous example of national meddling with their traditional prerogative of treating the blacks as they pleased. Even worse, it was widely believed that if blacks and whites were not rigidly segregated racial miscegenation would result. This view was ironic, considering the enthusiasm with which many Southern white men had sought black women; but it nevertheless was a strong factor in the mind of the region.

The stage was thus set for conflict, which was not long in coming. The first contested implementation of the court order came at Little Rock, Arkansas, in 1957, and these actions of the federal government were protested in the cartoons of the Memphis newspaper. The desegregation movement continued; and by the beginning of the presidential campaigns of 1960, it was apparent that the segregationist South could not expect public sympathy from either political party. This lack of support was especially bitter to the white South, for it saw the entire racial conflict as being a Communist plot. The Cal Alley cartoon of April 12, 1960, expressed this view.

Although the first battles in the struggle for racial equality took place in the South, a change occurred by the middle of the 1960's as unrest and rioting spread to cities in other parts of the nation. These events gave the Memphis cartoonist an opportunity to denounce militant black leadership and to extol more conservative Negroes such as Booker T. Washington, George Washington Carver, W. C. Handy, and Ralph Bunche.

Like many other Memphians, Cal Alley had a strong interest in the state of Mississippi. Long known as the deepest part of the deep South, the Magnolia state was a symbol as well as a reality, and one of the more interesting aspects of Memphis was its proximity to this quintessential part of the South. Mississippi was also in the trade area of Memphis and *The Commercial Appeal*; and even before the era of William Faulkner, close commercial and social connections had existed between the Tennessee city and its southern neighbor. Events in Mississippi consequently received frequent attention in the Cal Alley cartoons. Occasionally critical, as when they dealt with outdated marriage and prohibition laws, the drawings usually revealed understanding of and sympathy with the state and its problems. For example, during the integration crisis at the University of Mississippi in 1962 and during the campaign by Northern civil rights workers in 1964 (in which three of them were murdered near Philadelphia, Mississippi), the cartoonist's sympathies were with the whites of the state.

Cal Alley also demonstrated an understanding of the more general changes that affected the entire South, rather than just his local area. In this connection he drew cartoons dealing with such matters as the decline of cotton in the region's economy and the increasing movement of the white South toward the Republican party, particularly during the administration of President Richard Nixon.

State politics naturally received some of the attention of *The Commercial Appeal's* illustrations; but this topic was obviously less interesting to the cartoonist, and probably to his audience, than political issues of local, regional, and national significance. In Tennessee gubernatorial campaigns the illustrations opposed former governor Gordon Browning in 1948 when he lost the support of Boss Crump, who had previously delivered to him 60,000 Shelby County votes. Again the newspaper was against him in 1954 when he ran against Frank Clement. The drawings also generally opposed more liberal candidates such as John J. Hooker, Ross Bass, Estes Kefauver, and Albert Gore. In addition, they parodied Tennessee's ancient constitution and criticized rural dominance of state politics and the so-called "fair trade law." The legislature, bound by tradition and vested interests to a relatively inactive and negative role, also received repeated ridicule. Perhaps the basic cause of state government's lack of interest was that it was positioned between a more colorful local government and a much more active and powerful national government.

August 27, 1946

NOT A BAD SUGGESTION

June 25, 1946

MAYBE WE'RE BROADCASTING THE FACT TOO MUCH

June 7, 1950

'THAT'S YOUR END, NOT MINE'

June 21, 1956

You'll Never Make It, Samson

August 6, 1957

About Face, Little Man!

June 23, 1949

IN THE 'CLUTCHES' OF THE LAW

October 14, 1958

As We Are Pictured To The World

May 18, 1954

Relax! He'll Drink When He's Ready

September 13, 1957

"They Can't Do This To Me!!"

September 26, 1957

They Cut Some Corners Getting There

October 3, 1957

HEEL

October 16, 1958

Hear Ye!

April 12, 1960

Not-So-Strange Magnetism

July 13, 1960

Doesn't He Know It Hurts The Whole Donkey?

May 23, 1961

Sucker Bait

June 12, 1963

He Threw It SOUTH

June 16, 1963

The Ugly American

INCITEMENT TO RACE HATE

August 18, 1963

These Did It By Themselves

June 21, 1966

"Stop, Look And Listen!"

September 29, 1966

Let Plain John Doe Try It

August 6, 1967

Nailed To The Cross

April 16, 1963
"Git Them Cotton-Pickin' Hands Off Me!"

May 30, 1965

"Hello, Dollar!"

February 9, 1950

GRINDING UP A FEW LIVES IN THE PROCESS

May 4, 1955

Not Bad For A Country Boy

September 29, 1962

Saturday Roundup

June 23, 1964

This Is Going To Be Interesting

February 4, 1966

"Dern It Guv'nor, You Startled Me!"

February 19, 1970

Summa Cum Laude

November 25, 1962

"What's <u>Happening</u> To Me!?"

April 16, 1970

As Far North As He Can Go

June 30, 1948

TOTIN' A BURNED OUT TORCH

July 22, 1954

It Won't Stick

January 31, 1960

Tippy Canoe . . .

July 9, 1966

Saturday Roundup

August 3, 1966

Clearly Posted

October 27, 1967

Did Someone Mention Brainwash?

November 6, 1949

First Step In Putting Shoes On 'Im — CATCH 'Im

February 5, 1961

You're Mighty Right We're "Up In The Air"

February 9, 1961

"I Got A License"

March 25, 1966

So Far, We Ain't Heard No Music

February 27, 1968

Hang On, John

August 8, 1970

Saturday Roundup

BROCK-O BUSTER?
WE'LL SEE

GO AHEAD, ASK HIM ---
"WHO'D YOU VOTE FOR?"

A RACE WHERE THE
SHERIFF IS "TWO JUMPS AHEAD"

I'LL TAKE MINE
WELL-DUNN!

The Kennedy Era

Cal Alley, like other Americans who lived through the domestic placidity of the 1950's, saw the nation veer toward a new and noticeably different course with the beginning of a new decade. This new course was initiated by an unusually young, talented, and attractive contender for the presidency, Senator John F. Kennedy of Massachusetts, whose youth and Catholicism made his nomination as the Democratic candidate a surprise to many citizens. At first the cartoons of the Memphis newspaper did not seem to take a serious view of Kennedy's actions, but his success was soon pictured as assuring the death of the original purposes of the Democratic party. Although his presence in Memphis during September, 1960, for a speech was greeted courteously, the position of *The Commercial Appeal* and its cartoonist was resolutely against the Massachusetts senator. He was pictured as an irresponsible spendthrift whose Keynesian economic ideas were likely to result in deficit budgets that would increase the national debt and impoverish future generations of Americans. More serious was the charge that Kennedy would be a cowardly leader unable to stand up to Nikita Khrushchev in the cold war rivalry between the United States and Russia. By November, 1960, Richard Nixon, who had previously not been a particularly favored character in the Memphis cartoons, was the choice for the presidency. Nixon's campaign was unsuccessful and the United States entered the era of the New Frontier.

There is a noticeable consistency in Cal Alley's cartoon representations of President Kennedy's New Frontier: They were uniformly opposed to it. Some aspects of this administration received special criticism, but none were attacked more vehemently than the handling of relations with Cuba. Upon assuming the presidency, Kennedy inherited from Eisenhower both a Cuban problem and a prepared plan for dealing with it. The problem had become apparent when Fidel Castro, a young guerrilla leader, seized control of the island and established a strongly nationalistic government. The Castro regime at first had considerable sympathy in the United States, but conflicts over the seizure of American owned investments and suspicions about Communist influence resulted in open enmity between the two nations. The heavily bearded Cuban leader was easy to characterize in cartoons and thus became an excellent subject for caricature. Cuba soon turned to Russia for assistance and became dependent on that nation for economic and military aid. In this manner a cold war outpost of Russian influence developed near the shores of the United States. In order to remove this challenge, the Eisenhower administration prepared a plan for an invasion of Cuba by anti-Castro refugees under the direction of the U. S. Central Intelligence Agency.

Accepting this plan, President Kennedy ordered the invasion of Cuba during April, 1960. Needless to say, the invasion had the enthusiastic support of the Memphis newspaper and its cartoons. But the high hopes for the invasion and the popular uprising it was supposed to encourage were frustrated, and the result was utter disaster for the invaders and embarrassment for the United States at the Bay of Pigs. Throughout the remainder of the Kennedy administration, Cal Alley considered the failure to overthrow the Castro regime one of the greatest mistakes of the nation's foreign policy. His drawings called attention to the Cuban danger to the U. S. Navy base at Guantanamo Bay, to the continuing dislike of the United States by Latin American countries, and to what he regarded as the failure of Kennedy's basic Latin American policy, the Alliance for Progress. He objected to student visits to Cuba and continued to urge a United States military invasion of the island.

It is a fair generalization that the Cal Alley policy of editorial cartooning was anti-New Frontier and anti-Kennedy administration in general; indeed, there was no other president during the Memphis cartoonist's career he so much criticized and so little admired. Some of the drawings were whimsical, such as the one of May 12, 1962, comparing the Democratic party's Billie Sol Estes Scandal with the Republican party's Sherman Adams scandal. Other sketches were humorous, such as the one of August 5, 1962, dealing with excessive government spending and the president's noticeably luxuriant hair. All of the caricatures, however, were basically anti-Kennedy. Certainly it was not difficult to be critical of the president and the entire Kennedy family. Their wealth, power, success, and outspoken liberalism aroused widespread dislike as well as admiration. Few American presidents have inspired such adulation and such hatred, polarizing the nation into groups of supporters and opponents. Like the Gracchi brothers of the Roman Republic, the Kennedy brothers brought both hope and fear to their nation. And like their earlier counterparts, the Kennedy brothers had violent ends to their careers. Their deaths softened the feelings of many of their opponents, including Cal Alley who paid posthumous tribute to both the assassinated leaders, John and Robert Kennedy.

July 15, 1960

End Of The Trail

August 7, 1960

"Work? Are You Kidding?"

September 21, 1960

Welcome, Jack . . . We're All Ears

November 1, 1960

Debtors' Prison

November 3, 1960

In Whose Hands Do You Want The Government?

June 21, 1960

Hogwash!

April 18, 1961

We'll Give Them A Hand - - A Big One

August 4, 1961

Sooner Or Later And Better Sooner

November 16, 1962

Don't Push Us, Samson

March 20, 1962

"Gracias, Senor - - Now I Scratch Your Back"

March 12, 1963

Jack's Bean Stalk

July 2, 1963

Like, Man, You May Find The Pad - - Locked!

May 12, 1962

Saturday Roundup

August 5, 1962

"Isn't He First?"

November 24, 1963

Godspeed

June 7, 1968

Profiles In Tragedy

Lyndon B. Johnson and The Great Society

The unexpected and untimely death of President John Kennedy on November 22, 1963, necessarily caused an abrupt transition of the presidency. Vice President Lyndon Baines Johnson, a colorful and complex Texan with a long record of successful legislative leadership, took up the reins of government. As president he initially displayed qualities of modesty, proclaiming that he merely wished to continue the policies of his assassinated predecessor. It soon became evident, though, that Lyndon Johnson had far too much pride to follow in the footsteps of any man, and was determined to place his own brand on national policy, both foreign and domestic. His towering ego and obvious ambition had made his acceptance of the vice presidency a surprise to some, and the limitations of that office had been a source of frustration to him. The presidency, which he had sought for himself in 1960, offered a prospect much more to his liking.

Since he assumed the highest office with little more than a month remaining before the beginning of a presidential election year, much of President Johnson's early activity was directed toward his forthcoming bid to win the office in his own right. By the beginning of 1964, Johnson's position in the party was consolidated and he could devote his attention to establishing his own political record prior to the national conventions and the fall elections. In the safety of this position Johnson was able to work constructively while the leading Republican candidates attacked one another. In a particularly bitter intra-party struggle, during which the more moderate G. O. P. contenders—Nelson Rockefeller, Richard Nixon, George Romney, and William Scranton—were all eliminated, the candidate occupying the most right-wing position of all, Senator Barry Goldwater of Arizona, emerged as the winner. The Arizona senator, whose conservative position was much liked in the South, was also respected by Cal Alley. Of the Republican candidates, Goldwater was apparently his first and Nixon his last choice.

The cartoonist's public endorsement for the election, however, was the choice of his newspaper, Lyndon B. Johnson. Goldwater's campaign, based more on principle than on political expediency, required him to take a stand so far to the right that most of the American political spectrum was abandoned to his opponent, thus assuring a Republican defeat. The cartoon of November 5, 1964, which outlined the extent of Goldwater's loss, also noted the departure of much of the previously solid South from the Democratic party.

President Johnson, whose political career had begun during Franklin Roosevelt's New Deal, replaced John Kennedy's New Frontier with an extensive and ambitious program of his own which took its place in American history as the Great Society. The legendary skill with which the Texas president could manipulate Congress stood him in good stead as he took the domestic legislation of his predecessor, which had been blocked in the legislative branch, and forced its passage. A torrent of legislation dealing with such subjects as civil rights, health, poverty, housing, and education was enacted under the president's forceful leadership.

None of the new programs of the Great Society escaped the Memphis cartoonist's attention, and very few of them escaped his sharp pencil. Cal Alley's distaste for the Great Society was almost as strong as it had been for the New Frontier. He considered the Johnson social legislation to be fiscally irresponsible. Moreover, it was directed mainly toward groups with which the cartoonist had little sympathy. Johnson had at first received rather favorable attention in *The Commercial Appeal*'s cartoons, perhaps because of his Southern origins and because he had seemed somewhat conservative—or at least moderate—in comparison with Kennedy. The drawings had an unusual degree of success in portraying Johnson. Cal Alley's portrait of him, emphasizing his facial characteristics of prominent nose, chin, and ears, was developed early and underwent little change during his entire political career. Also parodied were the president's exaggerated public piety and unctuousness, as well as his penchant for managing the news to satisfy his desire for approval.

The Johnson administration, having received endorsement of such landslide proportions in the election of 1964, ended in ironic tragedy. But this debacle was not caused by any of the costly domestic programs so criticized in the Memphis cartoons. Nor was it caused by public scandal, although the Bobby Baker affair was embarrassingly close to the president himself and was probably more serious than those involving Sherman Adams and Billie Sol Estes during the two preceding administrations. The downfall of LBJ and his great society was caused by a failure in foreign affairs. Cal Alley's cartoon of December 30, 1965, in which the president's dance with a young lady at the Great Society Ball is interrupted by a skeletal apparition of a soldier from Vietnam, was much more prophetic than even the cartoonist realized. Although the fact was slow in becoming apparent, something was happening that would drive the Johnson administration from power, shatter the Democratic party, and divide the American people more than they had been divided since the anti-slavery crusade a century before.

This division of the American people was not as disturbing to Cal Alley as the methods by which protesters expressed their dissent from the government's policy toward Vietnam and the treatment of Negroes. The 1960's was a turbulent decade by any comparison, but one unusual development was the widespread public use by aggrieved groups of the tactics of nonviolent resistance to authority. Drawing from the teachings of Mohandas Gandhi and Martin Luther King, this technique relied on collective, symbolic, public, and peaceful, but occasionally obstructive gestures of dissent. Featuring boycotts, strikes, marches, and demonstrations, these activities did sometimes become involved in violence which could be started by police, angry onlookers, or by uncontrolled members of the protest group itself.

First used widely by Negroes in their civil rights struggle during the early years of the decade, the techniques of mass public protest were by the mid-1960's adopted by young white Americans to protest the war in Vietnam. Many citizens, especially older and more conservative ones, were deeply shocked by this phenomenon, particularly since it was used by people with whose ideas they disagreed. Cal Alley's cartoons dealing with the protest movements were outspoken and consistent. In what was certainly the majority viewpoint of his city and region, he caricatured the black and student demonstrations as thoroughly misguided and contemptible. They were pictured as being alien to the American tradition. In fact, he felt they were directed by an international Communist conspiracy and therefore to be opposed by all patriotic Americans.

January 5, 1964

Meanwhile, Back At The Ranch . . .

June 10, 1964

"Let's One Of You And Him Fight"

October 18, 1964

'Now, Coach?'

November 5, 1964

"I Never Woulda Believed It"

August 12, 1965

"WHA-A-T!!?"

October 31, 1965

The Melancholy Days Are Come

April 26, 1966

The Great "Spendgali"

September 7, 1966

Jes' A Plain Old-Fashion Circuit Rider

November 14, 1967

Again!!?

November 29, 1967

Going For "Broke" Here, Too?

January 8, 1966

Saturday Roundup

January 19, 1968

The Corn Was As High As An Elephant's Eye

February 18, 1962

Anybody You Know?

July 11, 1963

"Profile In Courage"

May 17, 1966

Boy Oboy Oboy, The Tramps Are Marching

May 24, 1968

Where Does He Get His Drive . . . His Push?

January 12, 1969

"Man, Dig This Crazy Book!"

June 14, 1970

The Only Way We'll Turn Our Back To The Flag

October 18, 1967

Tramp, Tramp, Tramps . . .

. . . THE *BOYS* ARE MARCHING . . .
MEN ARE STANDING FIRM!

December 30, 1965

"May I Cut In?"

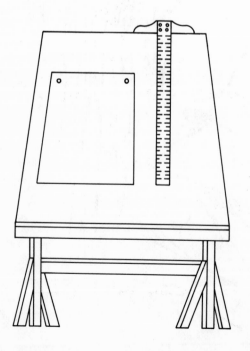

Vietnam

By the middle of the 1960's it was clear that the nation was again engaged in a war. But there were many things about this war that were not at all clear. Probably one of the most confusing and misunderstood of all the nation's wars (although no declaration of war was ever made), this conflict developed without the understanding of the people of the United States. There seemed to be no one able to explain to the public just when the war had started, why it was being fought, or exactly who the enemy was. Indeed, members of Congress seemed to be only a little less mystified than their constituents about it. The surprise which was felt by many citizens at finding the nation in a war in Southeast Asia was not shared by Cal Alley.

American involvement in the area, which developed slowly and fitfully through the administrations of several presidents, attracted attention in *The Commercial Appeal*'s cartoons in its initial phases. As early as May, 1953, these drawings took note of the conflict of Communist and American interests in Indochina. From this time onward Cal Alley maintained a continuing interest in the development of U. S. aims in that area. During these years he watched a steadily growing American presence in Vietnam. President Eisenhower, after the fall of Dien Bien Phu in 1954, provided the pro-U. S. government in South Vietnam with large amounts of aid and with the assignment at first of civilian advisers, whom he later replaced with 5,000 military personnel. Inheriting this policy, President Kennedy continued the program of aid and increased the number of military advisory personnel to 17,000. Despite Kennedy's belief in the importance of strategic interests in Indochina, his actions there attracted little attention among the American people.

By the summer of 1964, the situation in Vietnam seemed to be deteriorating, in spite of all that the United States had done. Premier Ngo Dinh Diem, the dictatorial but pro-American ruler of South Vietnam, had been killed in a coup and the government had fallen into a state of chronic internal crisis. Meanwhile, the successes of Vietcong guerrillas had increased to such an extent that the survival of the U. S. supported regime in Saigon was doubtful. In the United States, President Johnson came under attack by the Republican candidate, Barry Goldwater, who accused the president of not using sufficient military force against the communists in Indochina.

This was the situation in August, 1964, when the president, in a speech generally accepted by Americans at that time as being true, announced that the U. S. Navy had been attacked by North Vietnamese torpedo boats in the Gulf of Tonkin. President Johnson, proclaiming that "peace is the only purpose of our course," ordered air attacks on North Vietnam and asked for the support of Congress. A joint resolution was quickly passed giving him authorization to take actions he considered necessary. The Gulf of Tonkin Resolution and the events surrounding it certainly mark a turning point in America's involvement in the war.

After this point the remainder of the Johnson administration was characterized by a continuing escalation (a word that acquired new meaning in the nation) of military intervention and action, accompanied by repeated public assurances of the president's devotion to, and his search for, peace. By July, 1965, American troop strength in Vietnam had reached 75,000; but rapid increases brought the total by the beginning of 1966 to 190,000, in addition to 60,000 men assigned to the 7th Fleet. These American increases were matched by corresponding escalations by the Vietcong and North Vietnamese. The result was that despite the great losses the Communists were reported to be suffering, an American victory seemed to recede farther and farther away and the outcome appeared more likely to be a stalemate.

As the struggle settled into the course that was eventually to make it America's longest war, it became apparent that the fighting in Vietnam involved special problems. It proved unexpectedly difficult to convince the rest of the world of the rightness of this crusade. Except for a few Asian client states from whom President Johnson was able to exact token participation, America's traditional allies were noted for their lack of support. To the even greater chagrin of the Johnson administration, widespread criticism of the war developed inside the United States. This protest involved many members of Congress, students, educators, and writers; but the information for these objectors was generally supplied by the press, which seemed to take particular delight in exposing the lies and blunders of the president and his civilian and military spokesmen.

While criticism of U. S. actions in Vietnam increased in the news media, Cal Alley gave steadfast support to the war. He considered it to be an involvement necessary to protect the rest of the free world and to stop Communist aggression before it overran other American allies. He saw his country's two major enemies, China and Russia, as being the real opponents in the war and felt that critics at home and allies abroad who refused to help were simply serving the purposes of these enemies. His support continued unquestioningly through 1967 as U. S. troop strength in Vietnam increased to 525,000 men and casualty totals on both sides also mounted.

It was not until the Vietcong Tet offensive in January, 1968, that there was any indication that Cal Alley's support of the war was less than complete. This campaign was no great military victory for the Vietcong forces; but it was a major psychological defeat for American leadership, exposing as a pattern of lies the pronouncements which had so optimistically been disseminated by the U. S. government. While the Memphis cartoonist continued as a conservative and a Southerner to support the war, his cartoons dealing with American leadership became increasingly critical. He caricatured Secretary of State Dean Rusk, Secretaries of Defense Robert McNamara and Melvin Laird, South Vietnamese leaders Nguyen Van Tieu and Nguyen Cao Ky, and the U. S. Army for its attempt to cover up the massacre of Vietnamese civilians at My Lai by Lt. William Calley.

Continued developments in Indochina gave Cal Alley little cause for optimism. He expressed doubt about the usefulness of the Paris peace talks which started in 1968, and in April of the next year he noted sadly that U. S. battle deaths had exceeded the total of the Korean War and were still increasing. His sense of patriotism was undiminished but he seemed to share some of the bitterness and frustration that was being felt by many Americans about the war that seemingly could neither be won nor ended. After Lyndon Johnson had been forced from the presidency, mainly because of the war, the Memphis cartoons expressed reservations about President Richard Nixon's military incursions into Cambodia and Laos. At the time of Cal Alley's death Vietnam had become America's third most expensive war in total human casualties, and it was still not over.

May 5, 1953

It Takes But A Small Stone To Start An Avalanche

May 8, 1954

Saturday Roundup

March 9, 1955

Another One Busted Loose

March 11, 1962

Well, Well—The Shoe's On The Other Foot!

CAL ALLEY

April 19, 1964

Portrait

February 19, 1965

"No Parachute?"

May 12, 1965

"Velly Good Amelican Speech! Velly Good!"

June 16, 1965

"Let Go? Are You Kidding?!"

June 18, 1965

This Is Negotiation, In A Way

September 30, 1965

Face Of The Enemy

November 21, 1965

The Attitude Seems To Be Universal

September 18, 1966

After Vietnam, The Next Course On His Menu

February 6, 1968

Literally Shot Full Of Holes

February 28, 1968

Middle Course

June 11, 1968

As If The War Isn't Bad Enough

June 13, 1968

"It's Still There . . . Merely Suspended"

January 17, 1969

"Now, About The Chairs!"

April 2, 1969

Past It And Still Going

September 26, 1969

Pentagonese Has Worsenized

February 27, 1970

Not The Way Out

June 13, 1970

Saturday Roundup

July 16, 1970

Clean Sweep?

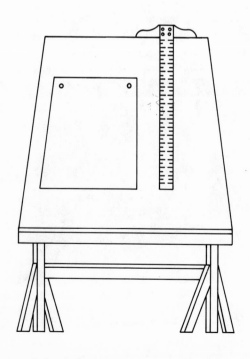

The Nixon Beginning

Few years in American history have held more surprising political changes than 1968. At the beginning of the year recent political precedents gave good reason to believe that the incumbent president, Lyndon B. Johnson, would undoubtedly win his party's endorsement to run for reelection, and that in all probability he would defeat whichever Republican challenger would run against him. The nation was therefore greatly surprised when the president appeared before a national television audience on March 31 to announce that he was retiring from politics and would not take part in the forthcoming presidential election. His reasons for reaching this surprising decision may never be known, but many Americans suspected that it was caused by the success of Senator Eugene McCarthy in the New Hampshire primary election and by the knowledge that the war had so reduced the president's popularity that he could not secure his party's nomination.

The announcement of Lyndon Johnson's decision to retire from politics left the outcome of the 1968 election in considerable confusion. Three men soon appeared as serious contenders for the Democratic nomination. Vice President Hubert H. Humphrey, even though his relations with LBJ had sometimes been difficult, soon emerged as the administration candidate. Senator Eugene McCarthy of Minnesota, who had been the first serious candidate to enter the race, was handicapped by limited financial support but had an enthusiastic corps of volunteer campaign workers, many of them young people. The most formidable candidate for the nomination, however, was Senator Robert F. Kennedy of New York, the younger brother of the assassinated John Kennedy. His political organization was large and well financed and he also commanded a large following of young people and minority groups. But the greatest strength of his campaign probably was his own charismatic personality and his inheritance of the great popularity with the public that his brother had enjoyed. Throughout the spring campaigning the Kennedy crusade gained strength, until his victory in the California primary on June 5 seem to have placed the nomination within his grasp. Then sudden tragedy struck: While celebrating his victory in Los

Angeles he was slain by Sirhan Sirhan, a Palestinian Arab who shot him because of his pro-Israel position.

The assassination of Robert Kennedy caused as great a change in the political scene as the withdrawal of Lyndon Johnson. With Kennedy gone, there was no one left with sufficient power to effectively challenge the administration. Thus the nomination at the Democratic convention in Chicago went to Hubert Humphrey. But Chicago was a tragedy for the party and for Hubert Humphrey. Much of the frustration that the nation felt about Vietnam found public expression as many demonstrators converged on Chicago and violent clashes occurred between them and the city's police. Tempers inside the convention were almost as rancorous, and when the session ended it was evident that the party was disasterously divided. The status of the party was appropriately represented by Cal Alley in his cartoon of August 28, 1968, depicting the Democratic donkey in battered condition.

In contrast, the Republican party suffered from no such division. Since their party had paid the high cost of polarization in the Goldwater campaign of 1964, the G. O. P. leaders were determined to avoid any ideological split within the party in 1968. Their convention was dull in comparison with that of the Democrats; but the Republicans emerged from their selection process united in the support of their nominee, Richard M. Nixon. Their choice for a vice presidential candidate, Maryland Governor Spiro Agnew, provided the substance for *The Commercial Appeal*'s cartoon of August 9, 1968, where his lack of recognition by the American people was parodied.

The presidential campaign of that year was certainly not one of the more exciting ones in American history. Richard Nixon campaigned against the alleged abuses of the Democratic administrations, promised action against the growing problems of crime and disorder that had frightened many citizens, and implied that he had a plan to end the war in Vietnam. Unlike his campaign of 1960 in which he was hampered by a lack of money, Nixon in 1968 had access to almost unlimited campaign funds. Hubert Humphrey was trapped in the dilemma of needing Lyndon Johnson's support to secure the nomination and being handicapped by this endorsement in the election when the voters considered him too much associated with Johnson's policies. He did not move far enough from the administration's positions to please many critics, but he did move far enough to lose the full and enthusiastic support of the proud Texas president.

The election was further complicated and made more colorful by the entry of the American Independent Party's candidates, Governor George C. Wallace and General Curtis E. LeMay. Since they appealed mainly to Southern voters with segregationist interests, their success was necessarily limited. Yet George Wallace received 9.9 percent of the popular vote, while 31.3 was received by Hubert Humphrey and 31.8 was received by Richard Nixon.

The Republican percentage of the electoral vote was considerably larger. Thus Richard Nixon assumed the presidency in 1969 having received a minority of the popular vote and having failed to secure a Republican majority in either house of Congress. He was the first president in more than a century to be inaugurated without his party's having a majority in at least one house of Congress. The new president faced grave problems of law enforcement, inflation, an unpopular war, lack of public faith in government, and a divided citizenry.

Cal Alley's portraits of Richard Nixon had always been rather ambivalent. They had recognized his success as a Republican party leader but had always presented him as a rather untrustworthy individual. This ambivalence continued to characterize his views of Nixon as president. The Memphis cartoonist was pleased with the new leader's presumed conservatism, hoping that it would herald an increased cooperation with conservative Southern Democrats; but he still considered himself at liberty to criticize aspects of the president's policy with which he disagreed. Cal Alley's respect for Richard Nixon apparently increased after the election, and the cartoons generally wished the new president well.

December 27, 1959

"I'm Runnin' Away—Hey! Didja Hear Me?'

November 27, 1966

"Stop Shaking That Tree!"

March 17, 1968

The Flower Children

July 16, 1968

"No Question As To Where It'll Be"

August 9, 1968

No. 2 Spot

August 28, 1968

And He Still Has To Take On An Elephant

November 8, 1968

Might Be A Cordial Relationship

January 7, 1969

Warming Up In The Bullpen

February 20, 1970

"We Need Help To Get It Together!"

June 4, 1970

"Howdy! How Y'all?"

June 18, 1970

"Steady, Boy . . . Steady . . . Easy, Now"

Personal Topics

There are probably few people whose work is more exposed to public examination than the editorial cartoonist of a major regional newspaper. Over a period of years his work may well be standard daily fare for several hundred thousand readers. Numerous topics of popular interest are likely to be presented; and in time his readers may be able not only to recognize the attitudes he expresses in his illustrations, but even to predict the position he might take on a particular issue.

Behind the cartoons which appear in a daily newspaper there is, of course, a cartoonist who is not only a professional artist, but also a person with individual interests and feelings. Cal Alley was such a person. He was able to put into his work such a personal touch that readers themselves became emotionally involved. Members of his reading public were often affected so strongly by the content of the cartoons that they were inspired to write about them to the editor of the newspaper or to the cartoonist himself. These letters often reflected the feeling that the writers had become personally acquainted with Cal Alley through his cartoons. Although his personality was usually not obtrusive in his work, selected examples of it do reveal much about him. Occasionally the characters in his drawings contained a special message for the cartoonist's family and friends, in addition to providing for other readers of the newspaper the necessary illustrations of his subject. Sometimes he used members of his family, especially the babies and children, as models for the characters in his drawings. His friends also were sometimes drawn, as is the case in the cartoon of June 11, 1953, in which his friend Lydel Sims, a columnist of the newspaper, appears. Familiar animals as well as people were placed in some of the sketches, such as the one of August 25, 1970, in which Junior, the Alley family dog, learns sadly of the beginning of school.

Other aspects of the cartoons also reflected personal interests of the artist. People he especially admired were frequently used as characters. Two of his heroes, Winston Churchill and Bernard Baruch, were used whenever possible to illustrate lessons for the newspaper's readers. As a cartoonist, he admired the resemblance of Winston Churchill to the symbolic British figure, John Bull.

Furthermore, his friends often heard him refer to quotations from Churchill's speeches.

Since he was strongly motivated by patriotism, one of Cal Alley's favorite cartoon characters was Uncle Sam. It is perhaps not surprising that he used himself as a model for the bearded symbol of the United States. In his drawings of Uncle Sam, his own distinctive nose and tall, trim figure may be seen.

Certain other preferences of the cartoonist may also be noted in his work, and his love of trees led him to place them often in the pictures. While spring was frequently noted in his drawings, his favorite season unquestionably was fall—especially October, the month of his birthday. On the other hand, there were certain things that he generally excluded from his work. Remarking that he was aware of the fact that many readers of the morning newspaper saw his cartoons during their breakfast, he limited his use of gory and unpleasant scenes, even in his most critical work.

Certain days were of personal interest and could often be expected to be noted in cartoons. For example, Columbus day on October 12 and Groundhog Day on February 2 were greatly favored, and other traditional holidays such as July 4, Thanksgiving, and Christmas were also regularly noted. The Thanksgiving cartoon of November 28, 1968, with the caption "We give thee thanks for what we have," appeared on his wedding anniversary and at a time when his daughter, Jehl, had recovered from near death following childbirth. Other holiday drawings with personal significance for the artist include one printed in color on the front page of the newspaper on the Fourth of July in 1968, which contained an idea suggested by his wife, and the Christmas Eve sketch of 1957, which accurately depicted his usual procrastination in purchasing gifts for her.

Reflected in the Cal Alley cartoons are many of the feelings experienced by ordinary people who lived in the area. Frustration with jobs, pleasure in the seasons, and the enjoyment of family love may be seen, as well as apprehension about the future, resentment of injustice, and the reassurance one may receive from religion. Disgust with those who ridicule accepted values, pride in his country and its accomplishments, and wistful sadness over the passing of time and life are also apparent.

Because of his arduous work schedule and because of his intense desire to retain his individuality of ideas, Cal Alley intentionally avoided becoming a "joiner" of service and fraternal organizations. He had an impulsive, gregarious, and sentimental nature. Quick-witted and keen of insight, he saw ordinary things from an unusual viewpoint. People never found being with him a dull experience. He enjoyed talking to people in all situations and also was in great demand to give "chalk talks"—running commentaries which he gave while sketching before his audience. These were always extemporaneous. His work constantly involved meeting people, including famous persons such as presidents and other celebrities who sometimes appeared in his cartoons. But he had an interest in, and appreciation for, the efforts of working people. This interest is illustrated by his cartoon of January 10, 1950, paying tribute to the linemen who had worked to repair the damage caused by an ice storm.

Perhaps Cal Alley's truest identification with most of his readers was that he shared the same patriotism and religious faith that they did. The drawings of April 16, 1954, and October 15, 1961, express the real feelings of the cartoonist toward these subjects. His readers generally agreed with and admired these positions, and in a "Volunteer State" known for its outspoken patriotism and in a "Bible Belt" area known for its religious zeal, Cal Alley's personal convictions coincided with those of his public. This was a happy arrangement, both for the cartoonist and for the newspaper's readers.

August 20, 1946

BACK FROM VACATION

April 10, 1948

SATURDAY ROUNDUP (TO HECK WITH IT)

May 9, 1948

The Best Years Of Our Lives

January 10, 1950

THE UNSUNG HEROES

June 11, 1953

How To Beat The Heat

April 16, 1954

So You Wonder If You'll Ever Make It?

October 26, 1955

"Go 'Way, Boy! You Bother Me!"

February 4, 1956

Saturday Roundup

BINGE-BOUND?

INTO THE ROUND FILE -
UNDER "B" -- FOR BOGUS

DECLARATION
OF WASHINGTON

SWEET MEMORIES
"WHEN WE WERE VERY YOUNG"

December 24, 1957

The Man Who Has Everything · · ·

--EXCEPT HIS WIFE'S PRESENT!

June 3, 1958

There Seems To Be A Similarity

October 30, 1958

Extremely Important Third Party

January 1, 1960

Leap Year

October 15, 1961

Hold Your Position!

June 21, 1964

Who Needs Ribbons And Bows And Boxes?

January 25, 1965

The Greatest Of That Few

June 22, 1965

Think Back And Remember

July 4, 1966

Let Freedom Ring!

December 17, 1966

Saturday Roundup

KEEPS POPPING UP

MEMORIES OF HIS BELOVED CREATIONS

WALT DISNEY

SOME THINGS LIVE FOREVER

TEAMSTER HOFFA

HORSE OF A DIFFERENT STRIPE

CHINESE ACCUSATIONS OF BOMBINGS

OLD PROVERB: "IF HEAT UNBEARABLE, GET OUT OF KITCHEN"

November 28, 1968

An Early Have-Not Nation

August 25, 1970

Dog Days

September 15, 1970

The Melancholy Days Are Come

AFTERWORD

After an association with Cal dating back to his prep school days it is especially gratifying to me to be asked to write this brief afterword.

Calvin Lane Alley was blessed with the quality of genius as were his parents before him. His mother, "Miss Nona," was the inspiration and sometimes collaborator with his father, James Pinckney Alley, Pulitzer Prize winning cartoonist of *The Commercial Appeal* and creator of a popular newspaper panel, "Hambone's Meditations."

The younger Alley was determined to someday succeed to the cartoonist's position of *The Commercial Appeal* and to that end worked his way through art school, including the Chicago Academy of Fine Arts where he became the friend of many renowned cartoonists, including Vaughn Shoemaker.

Cal's style and pen techniques followed closely those of his esteemed father. He originated a widely-syndicated newspaper strip "The Ryatts" and won a number of cartoonists' awards including the Sigma Delta Chi award for editorial cartooning in 1955.

He had an infinite capacity for indignation against malfesance and misfeasance in the handling of public affairs. It was matched by a gentle humor that often manifested itself in his drawings and his "originals" were the proud possessions of presidents and other individuals prominent in business, political or economic affairs.

He was the husband of Geraldine Jehl Alley and father of Calvin Lane Alley, Jr., Richard Wesley Alley, Mrs. Harry Petrie, Mrs. Harmon Williams and Mrs. Joseph Palvado, Jr. who were the principals of "The Ryatts."

His devotion to his family and his work left little time for leisure. There are those of us who would protest that he was driving himself too hard, but he was his own man and would not countenance any talk of assistance, even though he was, in reality, pursuing two careers as cartoonist for the newspaper and a successful syndicate author and illustrator.

There were several warnings of physical stress before the full impact of his fatal illness struck November 10, 1970, ending a brilliant career at the age of 55.

Frank R. Ahlgren
Editor, *The Commercial Appeal*
November 1936-December 1968

BIBLIOGRAPHICAL NOTE

The following suggestions are included for those who may wish to do additional reading about the topics mentioned in this book. The basic source of course, is *The Commercial Appeal* itself. Fortunately copies have been reproduced on microfilm and are available in a number of places, including the John Willard Brister Library of Memphis State University and the Cossitt-Goodwyn Library of the Memphis Public Library System. These newspapers contain the entire collection of Cal Alley editorial cartoons which appeared in Memphis. It was from this collection that those used in *Cal Alley* were selected. The features "Hambone" and "The Ryatts" are also available from the years in which he drew them in these papers. Additionally, the newspapers contain the news reports read by those who followed Cal Alley's work, as well as expressions of public opinion such as editorials and letters to the editor. Similar information is available in the microfilmed copies of the Memphis *Press-Scimitar*. Many of Cal Alley's cartoons are in the possession of his family, even though his generosity with the originals has caused those surviving to be widely dispersed.

There are several useful histories of Memphis. The best one, published before Cal Alley started his editorial cartooning in Memphis, is *The Biography of a River Town, Memphis: Its Heroic Age*, by Gerald M. Capers, Jr. (Chapel Hill, 1939). A newer edition of Capers' book, published in New Orleans in 1966, contains only one essay not included in the original edition. Two older works which provide useful background material are John McLeod Keating's *History of the City of Memphis and Shelby County, Tennessee* (3 vols.; Syracuse, 1888) and James Davis' *History of Memphis* (Memphis, 1873). Davis' history was reprinted by the West Tennessee Historical Society (1972). Information about specific parts of Memphis history may be found in Shields McIlwaine's *Memphis Down in Dixie* (New York, 1948), and in two books by William D. Miller, *Memphis During the Progressive Era, 1900–1917* (Memphis, 1957), and *Mr. Crump of*

Memphis (Baton Rouge, 1964). An excellent history of *The Commercial Appeal* is Thomas H. Baker's *The Memphis Commercial Appeal: The History of a Southern Newspaper* (Baton Rouge, 1971). Most of this account deals with the period before Cal Alley became editorial cartoonist for the newspaper. An adequate history of Memphis during the last quarter of a century is yet to be written.

Historical information about the Memphis area has also been gathered in other sources. The West Tennessee Historical Society *Papers*, a professional journal of high quality, has been published annually since 1947 and contains articles on many topics of local interest. An extensive collection of tape recorded interviews, many of them with people from the Memphis area, has been developed by the Oral History Research Office of Memphis State University. These interviews, some of which have been transcribed, are kept with the store of regional materials in the Mississippi Valley Collection of the university's library. The Memphis Room of the Memphis Public Library system also has a useful collection of local historical records.

The best source of general information about Tennessee is Stanley J. Folmsbee, Robert E. Corlew, and Enoch L. Mitchell, *History of Tennessee* (Knoxville, 1969). This history was originally published (New York, 1960) in four volumes. Two older but useful accounts are Philip M. Hamer (ed.), *Tennessee: A History 1673–1932* (4 vols.; New York, 1933), and Thomas P. Abernethy, *From Frontier to Plantation in Tennessee: A Study in Frontier Democracy* (Chapel Hill, 1932). This study has been reprinted several times. There are several good histories dealing with the South as a whole. Among the most useful of these are Thomas D. Clark (ed.), *The South Since Reconstruction* (New York, 1973), W. J. Cash, *The Mind of the South* (New York, 1941), and C. Vann Woodward, *Origins of the New South* (Baton Rouge, 1951).

Other interesting books containing cartoons, some of them contemporary with Cal Alley's life, include The Editors of the Foreign Policy Association, *A Cartoon History of United States Foreign Policy Since World War I* (New York, 1967), William Cole and Mike Thaler (ed.), *The Classic Cartoons* (Cleveland, 1966), and William Henry Mauldin, *I've Decided I Want My Seat Back* (New York, 1965). Histories of the press in the United States are Edwin Emery and Henry L. Smith, *The Press and America* (Englewood Cliffs, New Jersey, 1954), and Frank L. Mott, *American Journalism: A History, 1690–1960* (New York, 1962).